D1231105

DON'T!

MICHAEL CRAUGHWELL

DON'T!

MISADVENTURES OF A SWORD GUY

MICHAELCTHULHU

trustees

DEDICATION

I would like to thank my friends and family,
without whom this book would have been finished a
lot sooner, and that's not a bad thing.

TABLE OF CONTENTS

INTRODUCTION

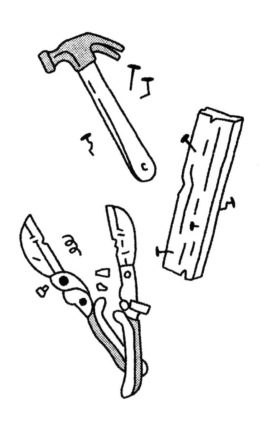

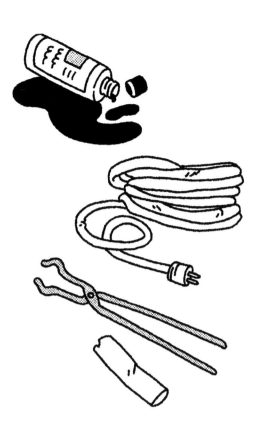

"ONLY A FOOL
LEARNS FROM HIS OWN
MISTAKES. THE WISE MAN
LEARNS FROM THE MISTAKES
OF OTHERS."

-OTTO VON BISMARCK

(ACCORDING TO SOME MEME I SAW
ON THE INTERNET)

LOOK AT ME opening up the whole thing with a quote, like a real book written by an adult! Please don't think I'm super into Otto Von Bismarck; to use a euphemism for "bad," he was a complicated figure. One sentence in and I sense I may have started an argument in some homes. I'll never know. Unlike my YouTube videos, books don't have comment sections. It's more the gist of the quote I liked rather than the speaker. It's basically the mission statement of this entire book. I got mangled, so hopefully you can learn from my mistakes.

I don't think I've ever owned a tool I haven't used to do something it wasn't supposed to do. Can you believe this book was originally pitched to me as a guide for you to do as I do? You shouldn't do as I do. No one should. This is more a set of cautionary tales. That sounds overly dramatic. I've never lost a limb or anything. I can still count to ten on my fingers, but I can probably count to eleven if I use the scars on my hands instead. The kid version of me probably thinks that sounds cool, but adult me would prefer to have the fine motor control back.

If you've just randomly picked this book up, then I guess I might have to back up a smidge. I make long-ass videos of myself making ridiculous fantasy weapons and upload them to YouTube. I have a hard time understanding the appeal my videos have, but I'm talking to my therapist about my appeal in general, so I might get to the bottom of it someday.

Some people are there to see the ridiculous weapons, obviously, and can't believe that someone made a real "functioning" version of BLANK from (insert name of video game/manga/movie/anime). Back in the day, I used to upload short videos of just the finished product smashing apart various targets while I struggled under the thing's ungainly bulk. That's the quote marks around "functioning." I've fallen into a niche where I only agree to make the ungainly weapons, so these things are 50 pounds on average, whereas a historical sword might be only 3 pounds—light enough to be wielded by a guy with a fedora.

The numbers are in though, and I think more people hang around for the process, because my process, like the weapons themselves and my sense of self-preservation, is extremely odd. I tend to do quite a lot with very basic tools. I love angle grinders. This MOSTLY isn't out of poverty but is instead the result of the way my relationship with making things began, leading to a lifelong set of destructively bad habits.

CHAPTER 1

LARVAL LEARNINGS: MY NOSE IS STILL CROOKED

I HAVE A VERY FOUNDATIONAL MEMORY from when I was seven or eight that has to do with my nascent desire to make all the stuff. We were too poor to have "the channels" (cable), but my poor ol' dad would sometimes get friends to record stuff off the channels, and then we'd watch it as tapes. I don't know how the economics worked out that VHS tapes and straining the relationships with friends and family who could afford cable was cheaper than actually getting cable, but somehow it worked out, I guess. My father also ran a pirate movie empire, so maybe that's how.

So anyway, I was watching some children's program, and there was a guy doing origami. Normally I would not have had the materials, but since this was a video recording, young me could pause the program and go get the things I needed. I was very excited. After gathering all the materials, I sat down to begin. This was going to be easy. The nice man in the video started in his soft children's presenter voice, "We begin by folding the piece of paper in half, right down the middle." Then he did. So, I paused the video, took my child hands and attempted to duplicate. It didn't fold straight down the middle. It was messed up and folded somewhat crookedly. I unfolded the paper, smoothed it out, and attempted it again. Still crooked. I tried a third and fourth time. All crooked.

Maybe I hadn't slept enough or needed food (I still have difficulty recognizing when I need food). For whatever reason, child-me couldn't cope with the fact that I wasn't able to fold the paper correctly, that I couldn't even get past step ONE of this process. I broke down in tears. Eventually my father came to check on me, but he didn't understand why not being able to fold a piece of paper perfectly in two could possibly be a cause for tears. This inability to empathize added to the sting and caused the incident to become a paragraph in this book thirty-three years later.

Looking back, I think my frustration was the gap between knowing what I wanted my hands to do and not being able to get my hands to do it. It might have been the first time I was face-to-face with the gulf between my ambition and my reach. I like to think that this incident was what led me to go on and develop the uncommon level of manual dexterity I have nowadays. A similar thing probably happens to other kids, and they decide that painting, model making, or origami is not for them. They move on, but obviously it was important to me that I WAS good at making things. Even at that young age, I mostly identified with the mad scientist or inventor characters in various kids' cartoons, so being forced to admit to there being limits for my pudgy digits was upsetting and led me down a path of wanting to become good at making things. I didn't have the same reaction to my poor physical ability, or my inability to carry a tune, or my social awkwardness.

It was the inability to fold a piece of paper cleanly in two that shook me and made me want to "git gud."

Cut to a few years later, and I have actually gotten somewhat good at making things. Somewhat good. I was about ten years old when the incident with the lean-to shed–type thing happened. It was built from random rotten sheets of plywood and such. I can't remember where I found them. My parents had bought me a toy tool chest, but with real working tools in it: a tiny hammer, a tiny saw, etc. It was probably one of the best things they ever got me, life direction-wise. I used the tiny hammer to punch the nails through the rotten wood I used for this shed/fort/hut thing, which was easy because, like I already noted, it was rotten. Having finished making this "monstrum," I wanted to know how sturdy it was. I climbed up on top of the roof. Gingerly, I tested my weight on it. Seeing as it was able to hold my weight standing still, I decided to see if it could take my weight while moving around just a little bit.

This is a bad way to test things, but the roof seemed like it could take me moving around a little. Then I started to move around a lot. Proud of my handiwork, I started to stomp on the roof, and from there, I tried jumping on the roof. Well, I say "jumping," but jumping implies that more than one jump occurred. One jump was all it took before the shed collapsed underneath me.

In the confusion of collapsing timber, some random piece of lumber was levered by my falling body, cartoon-style, directly into my face. I remember the white-hot pain and confusion. I ran into the house. My parents couldn't decide whether to comfort me or to scold me, so they settled on a mishmash of the two. If my kid had just broken their nose, I probably would have taken them to the hospital, but the 1980s were a simpler time. My nose reset itself ever so slightly off. I still notice it in the mirror sometimes, but either it's not actually that bad or my eye software has gotten used to it and edits it out.

Sometimes I will watch my own son climbing stuff and trying stunts with impromptu trapeze equipment he has made from ropes and such that he has found. Occasionally, rarely, he falls and hurts himself. But he always climbs back up the ladder or tree, sometimes with the dried tears from the previous failure still visible on his face. I was like that with making stuff. Still am. Other than an injury that makes it physically impossible, I don't think I will ever stop making stuff.

Neither of my parents were really good at making things, and I don't think they really understood the extent of the urge in me. That toy tool chest they got me represented the only toolbox in the house. Ireland is starting to have more of the DIY culture America has had for a long time, but it was barely existent in the '80s when I was small, especially not in the tightly packed row houses I grew up in. Child-me would often come across American books about making stuff where they'd tell you how easy it was to acquire all the necessary materials at your local hardware store. Ha! My father was definitely not a DIY type of guy. He once knocked a spectacular crater in the tiny guest-bedroom wall trying to hang a shelf. To be fair, drilling into masonry can be tricky, but unlike me, I'm not sure he knew that before he started. I mostly KNOW how dangerous a lot of the stuff I attempt is before I try it, but then I do it anyway. How does the meme go? *The risk I took was calculated, but man, am I bad at math.*

A core memory from my young teen years is a car breaking down outside of our family home. The stranded motorist asked my father if there were any tools he could borrow. Dad disappeared inside our house for a while and emerged with a hammer and a hacksaw. Luckily, by the time he had arrived with the implements, the guy had figured out how to restart his engine by himself and made his escape. I asked my father afterwards what he thought one might do to fix a car engine with a hammer and a hacksaw? He didn't know. I don't want to give the impression my father was dull. He comes across as quite smart and charming. Just don't ask him with help assembling your Ikea chair if you want to be able to sit down anytime in the next week.

I used that hammer and hacksaw; I used them an incredible number of times. There were a lot of fantasy and sci-fi films in the '80s: *Krull, Conan the Barbarian, Red Sonja, The Dark Crystal.* While young nerd-me loved them all, I was powerless to recreate the artifacts from them. But then there were the *Mad Max* films. They presented a future where the bombs had dropped, and everyone was rifling through the past and trying to make stuff with whatever was lying around. I COULD emulate that. The postapocalyptic future looked a lot like the floor of my bedroom, with random steel scraps collected from the side of the road. I didn't have to have a Dwarven Forge® in the heart of a mountain to make things. A dusty patch of ground and an old discarded tire would suffice.

Unlike weapons, I could make armor without people becoming too alarmed. (I did make weapons too. Half of a pair of broken shears were wired into what you guys call a "closet rod" to make a spear-type thing. The parents were not super thrilled.) I acquired road signs to make armor, sometimes not even illegally: A random badnik did me the favor of stealing the sign already and dumping it in a bush by the nearby train tracks after the funniness of having stolen it wore off. Using the hacksaw to cut shapes out of the road signs was a different type of sweaty solo work for a lonely teenager. Then it would be the hammer's turn to use masonry nails to drive holes in the plates so I could then wire all the plates together. Pipe insulation for padding was held in place with electrical tape, and then black spray paint finished it. The result looked awful, just like something from *Mad Max*. When I think of all the hardship I could have avoided if someone had bought me a drill or a jigsaw, I shudder. The drill my father used to LARP (live action role-play) Minecraft in the guest bedroom was borrowed, so that was off-limits. My smashed fingers built character, I suppose.

At around age sixteen, the Pound Shop Katana was another pivotal moment for me, but probably not for the reason I thought it would be ("Dollar Store Katana" for those of you who can get a gun more easily than a doctor). Why my mum let me buy it, I will never know. A tang is the extension of a sword or knife's blade that goes through and to the end of the handle. I don't think my Mum knew the Dollar Store Katana had a "false tang," but who knows?

I tend to cringe pretty hard when I see photos of guys with trench coats and katanas on the Internet because I was a hair's breadth away from being one of them. Luckily, my katana broke. The balsa wood handle fell apart to reveal that instead of a full tang, it had about an inch of thin nubby steel glued into a handle. Ideally, the tang goes all the way to the back of the handle (the pommel), but a lot of cheaper swords will have what's known as a "rat tail tang." A rat tail tang occurs when a person in an impoverished country is forced by global capitalism to spend all day spot welding lengths of threaded bar to the ends of blades so handles can be screwed on. If they ever stop, there is a significant risk they will starve to death. Well, that child laborer must have figured out how to escape the factory or died still shackled to his workstation while no one noticed because when my DOLLAR STORE KATANA fell apart, it didn't even have the length of threaded bar on there.

Years later, I often get messages from guys who ask if my swords are "full tang." I suspect it's because they've had experiences just like my own, and they can't tell the difference between my properly welded steel handles and nubs of steel glued to the cheapest wood available by just looking. Maybe I give people a hard time about this. I am a very visual person. I remember in my early twenties two friends of mine made an impressive short by rotoscoping (drawing on top of) individual frames of footage to make a lightsaber fight the original 1970s way. It was less than a minute long and took them months. When I showed it to my dad, I couldn't understand why he didn't find it impressive. It transpired that he couldn't actually SEE the lightsaber effect when I asked him what he thought of the short; "Those are those lightsaber toys you get down at the Pound Shop. They have the light in and everything."

But getting back to my broken katana, I knew I was never going to convince my mother to let me buy a second one, not after she witnessed how much sliced-up fruit was lying around the yard as a result of the first one. I had to fix it myself somehow. Yet again, my only tools were a hammer and a hacksaw. I don't know how long it took me to find a piece of aluminum pipe through scavenging, but eventually I found a fairly beefy pipe that the "dehandled" sword blade would fit down. If I had any advice for young Mike here, it would be that I didn't need to wait to find one that fit precisely. I could have found one that was slightly smaller, then hammered it on the concrete outside until the blade fit down it, and that oval pipe would have been a better handle anyway.

The next step was cutting two short pieces from a length of copper pipe I'd found. These ones I did flatten a bit; it was the only way to get them in the aluminum pipe on either side of the sword blade. Then it was time for the other half of all my tools: I hammered the copper pipes, sandwiching the blade down into the aluminum pipe, until the blade was secure. I still have that sword. It's in my father's attic in Ireland, and it is the ugliest thing you ever saw, but the blade never fell out of the handle, despite years of slashing fruit out of the air like the lonely neckbeard I was.

Speaking of being a lonely neckbeard, the Irish high school equivalent was definitely a rough ride for me. As an adult, I got diagnosed with some flavor of ADHD, but back in the day, ADHD was just "being lazy." I was too unfocused to do class work, but too nerdy to be interested in sports and such. There was a group of misfits I hung out with, but it wasn't by choice. All the kids no one else wanted to hang out with were squished together into one ship-of-the-damned type of arrangement. This will sound really dark, but the Columbine shooting was actually good for me. I started wearing a trench coat style to school shortly after and went overnight from being a target of torment to someone people were worried about (in case you are too young or don't remember, the early narrative with those assholes is they were bullied over the edge. This turned out to not be true; they were just assholes). Instead of people just hating me, they were now slightly afraid of me, and that was definitely an improvement, even though that identity further hurt my chances of getting along with anyone.

Back to the subject of ADHD ruining my academic chances, when I look back at the amount of time the sword took to fix, I am shocked I was able to focus long enough to do it. There is a concept in ADHD that you are able to hyperfocus on tasks to the point of ignoring your bodily needs. I certainly fit that bill. Actually, brb. Gotta pee real bad.

In the '90s, Ireland finally had money, and the PlayStation 1 (PS1) was out. So, I severely damaged my academic career playing *Final Fantasy VII (FFVII)* and *Soul Blade*. Both games gave me a fetish for huge swords, which would later launch my career. But somehow, while my homework lay discarded and undone on the floor because I was getting all five endings in *Silent Hill*, I found the time to spend hours cutting copper pipe with a totally blunt hacksaw blade. I don't think there's anything I would spend as long doing for such little reward in my adult life.

Here started a struggle that was both a blessing and a curse for the rest of my life. I think a lot of people like watching my YouTube channel because of how much I do with so little, BUT this attitude of squeezing the maximum amount of utility out of everything was born out of a kid in a bedroom in Ireland who didn't have access to materials and who would literally reuse electrical tape by putting it back on the roll after unwrapping it from the previous project.

This has haunted me to this day, and now as an adult, when time is money, I still spend way too much time doing everything by hand with the simplest of tools. I have a TIG welder now, but I should have had one a decade earlier. The same can be said of the plasma cutter, which I only have because Hollywood bought one for me. I look at other YouTubers spitting out one video a week and think of myself as a failure because I'm still not comfortable splashing out loads of money on fancy tools.

I get genuine enjoyment out of spending all day fixing a tool that would cost $30 to replace. It makes me sad to throw stuff in the trash, even though I know that would be a better use of my time in 90 percent of situations where I'm considering patching a break in an extension cord for the tenth time. All this can be directly traced back to a crooked-nose kid in row houses in mid-'80s Ireland who had no ability to go buy new nails but had the time and inclination to use a concrete block and hammer to straighten out the nails he did have. Over and over again.

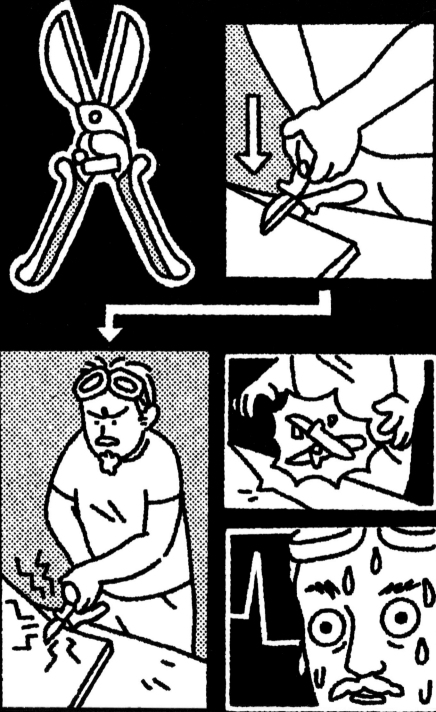

CHAPTER 2

ART COLLEGE AND THE CRUSHING OF MY BALLS

IT'S HARD TO EXPRESS what a shock to the system it was going to art college.

The all-boys Catholic Secondary School (high school) I went to was very "institutional," which is code for "prison-like." Not much input was required from me about . . . anything . . . and Ireland was kind of like that on a nationwide level. Hibernia always scores super high whenever anyone bothers to measure "quality of life" across different countries, but whenever I go back there, I look around at the endless row houses and the gray sky and I really, really hope that it's not crushing homogeny that turns out to be the ultimate secret to society-wide contentment. I remember reading someplace that when an infant starts forming memories is directly related to how much independence the child is given. I was not given any. I have no childhood memories earlier than about age eight.

I still think I was a little bit in this weird, not-quite-conscious pre-person state all the way to age eighteen, when I landed in college. Either that or I mostly lived in my head because no one criticized what I was doing there. That might sound like a win, but that is not healthy either, guys. You need to find your tribe to call you out when you're spouting–or thinking–bullshit. Some of the most cringe-inducing videos on the Internet are the result of lonely young men who spent too much time with only themselves for company. (I would once again like to thank the Internet for not having the ability to easily upload videos until after I was mostly an adult.)

The brick-in-the-wall, not-quite-person, walking-around-in-a-daze image of myself I'm presenting may not quite gel with the weird kid from high school you just saw. The misfit in me was definitely struggling to break free, but it was an uphill battle the entire way. And for sure it was easier to be weird by myself in my bedroom than anywhere outside. But art college was bizarro world. Whereas before I adopted a weirdo-in-a-trench-coat vibe as a sort of defense mechanism to keep people away, in art college it had the opposite effect. I was not used to getting positive feedback. I guess this is where I learned I am an extrovert, but only among groups of other weirdos. A selective extrovert; a "selectrovert." (Wait a second, the Internet is tapping me on the shoulder . . . "ambivert?" Why would you go with that when "selectrovert" is right there for the taking?)

I was immediately distracted by two things in art college: ladies and power tools. Herein, we will mostly discuss my adventures with the latter. It's almost impossible to imagine now, but when I started art college in the year 2000, I knew I loved making things, but I had almost zero knowledge about any tools other than the random paltry selection I'd seen around at home. Without the Internet, the only way for me to know something existed was to wander across a real one or to see a picture in a book. And there were crap-all books out about how to do what I do. (Hey! Is this one of those books now?)

I actually did pretty badly with the coursework for art college because of the two aforementioned distractions: girls and the tools in what was known as "the sculpture yard." It might have been a yard at some point. It was a roofed-over indoor space by the time I was there. A sculpture warehouse. Looking back, getting distracted by that stuff in the sculpture yard was probably the best use of my time there. The actual coursework was largely pointless and designed to keep us from using up too much of the material resources of the place, which is fair. Safe to say that 100 percent of what I made there was garbage. If I had made it from paper instead of steel, that would probably have been less wasteful. So, much like what turned out to be a disastrous choice in ladies due to inexperience, I also chose poorly when it came to the tools and wound up crushing my testicles the first week I was there.

I had never seen "tin snips" before. They're basically giant scissors. Think a large heavy snub-nosed pair of scissors. It's hard now to imagine how excited I got about the tin snips. Cutting metal—any kind of metal—was a giant pain in the butt at home. I would spend all day with a hacksaw. The tin snips made cutting thin metal super easy. But like any tool I've ever interacted with, I imme-

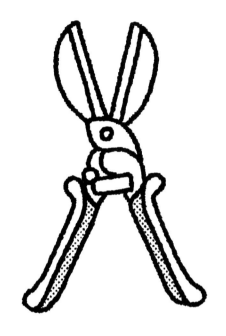

"...THE HANDLES OF THE
SNIPS COLLAPSED IN ON
THEMSELVES, EXPLOSIVELY
CLANKING INTO EACH OTHER
LIKE REUNITED LOVERS AT
AN AIRPORT. EXCEPT FOR
THE LAST TIME, WHEN ONE OF
MY TESTICLES GOT IN THE
WAY OF THEIR REUNION."

diately started to use them beyond the scope of what they were designed for. There might be a pair of tin snips out there that can easily cut 1-mm-thick mild steel. The ones I found could not. No one had shown me what an angle grinder was yet.

I found that I could torture the snips through the thicker material if I put an unreasonable amount of force on the handles, more force than I could muster by just holding the snips in my hands. I placed the snips upright and sideways on a table and, securing the piece I wanted to cut, pressed my full body weight down on the handle NOT wedged against the table. The problem with this arrangement was that in order to get my full body weight over the handles, my body had to be unreasonably close to the precariously balanced snips. It's a wonder what happened next didn't happen sooner because I spent like an hour cutting stuff that was too thick with this method before the inevitable occurred.

If you put your arms straight down in front of you and your hands one over the other, like you're doing CPR, you might notice that your hands wind up hovering over your crotch. That's exactly where the open handles of the snips were. As I pushed down with all of my force, the thick material would protest before giving way with a boom as the handles of the snips collapsed in on themselves, explosively clanking into each other like reunited lovers at an airport. Except for the last time, when one of my testicles got in the way of their reunion.

I instantly broke out in a cold sweat, the kind of sweat that lets me know some medical emergency has just occurred. I knew I was in trouble when I didn't feel any pain. I was a little nauseous maybe. And thirsty. And cold. But not actually in any pain. I was alone at the time, so I don't know if I went pale, but I suspect I may have. I had a bit of a sit-down. Years later, I learned that these are the symptoms of shock. My "brovary" eventually did start to hurt, thank goodness, and then continued to hurt for maybe a week. I am ashamed to say that young me was such an idiot for not thinking to go to the hospital. But also, young me healed much better and faster than current me, I guess, because the moron who crushed his balls went on to father two children with no problems. I wear a big heavy leather apron these days. It is the last piece of PPE (personal protective equipment) I remove when working with any kind of tool with a kick, and now you know why.

When my balls healed, I still needed to cut the steel. And this time I tried asking one of the sculpture technicians about it. So, that's how an eighteen-year-old, who had never handled a power tool in his life, was handed a 9-inch angle grinder and told to work away. Angle grinders are probably one of the simplest tools on the planet. It's just an electric motor with a set of bevel gears to rotate the spinning action of the motor by ninety degrees (the "angle" in "angle grinder"). There're handles to hold it. A switch. And a way to lock various types of discs into it. That's it. Its entire job is to spin.

They come in various sizes though, the two most common sizes being 4½ inches and 9 inches, which refer to the size of disc they take. There are loads of types of ammo for grinders, but the most common type is generally a hard disc of abrasive compound that's fat for grinding lumps off steel or thin for cutting through steel. It's insane that young me was handed the larger one. An inexperienced user can literally be dragged around by them. When you turn the grinder on, you can feel the force of a 9-inch disc spinning between 6,000 and 7,000 rpm trying to pull the grinder out of your hands. And that's before you've even touched the steel with the spinning death disc.

Years later, when I did an actual welding course, I finally got a safety lecture about grinders. In the town where I grew up, there's a racecourse. Part of the safety lecture was telling us about the guy who died when they were building the track. He was using a 9-inch grinder to cut the end of an I-beam (steel girder). A guy in a forklift reversed into the other end of the girder, twisting the beam while the disc was halfway through it. One of the key features of the standard cutting disc is that it's brittle, so it exploded. The disc, no longer round and having a jagged edge, was now impossible to control and sank thirstily into this poor guy's inner thigh, hitting an important artery. It must have looked like something from a Sam Raimi movie. He was dead before anyone could do anything.

Cut to a couple of decades later and eighteen-year-old me had just been handed the same tool with no guidance beyond wearing goggles and clamping the piece I'm working on down to a table. That's not terrible advice, but nowhere near comprehensive enough. I barely mention things like goggles and clamps in my videos because I foolishly assume they're self-evident, but writing this, ruminating on my idiot younger self, I realize these might require emphasis. The goggles I was thrown should only ever have been thrown away. While the point of safety glasses is to stop stuff from hitting your eye, there must be an interesting intersection of lines on some graph where it shows a point after which it gets more dangerous to wear them. That point is where the goggles are so scratched you CAN'T ACTUALLY SEE OUT OF THEM. The pair I caught out of midair was basically opaque. As I put them on and fired up the grinder, I got nervous and sweaty, so the goggles fogged up even more. I was as blind as an elderly motorist ploughing through a crowd of pedestrians. Keep your safety glasses scratch-free and tight to your face, kids. It's a miracle I'm here to write this.

Luckily, and this was mostly luck, I did actually have the work piece clamped to the table properly. If I had not, there is a serious chance I would have died that day. A loose piece, grabbed awkwardly by a grinder, can fly across a room and *Final Destination* whoever is standing in the way (pretend I used *The Omen* as a verb there if you're much older than I am. I don't know what the zoomer equivalent would be, but I'm sure it will make me unfairly and irrationally annoyed).

I could see a LITTLE better once I actually started cutting, thanks to all the sparks. I think the sparks are the thing that really spooks first-time users of angle grinders. In the real world, we tend to think of something throwing off tons of sparks and fire as indicative of either something going disastrously wrong or fireworks. I like to think of grinders as fireworks because of the spark show and the noise! Angle grinders are extremely noisy in an enclosed space. I was not handed earmuffs, but I should have been. Nor was I given a respirator. While "dose makes the poison," and using a grinder every now and again won't kill you, this was the start of me spending the rest of my life grinding. If there's a fine dust that you can inhale a lot of without eventually getting cancer, I've never heard of it. I had snot for days after.

I realized after I was done that it was probably a mistake to try this while wearing my long neckbeard coat.

It probably looked pretty funny, but if the sparks had lit up the coat . . . Well, the real tragedy is this was long before everyone had a camera in their pocket, so the ensuing enflamed flailing wouldn't even have been on film. After what felt like a lifetime, I finally cut through the sheet of steel. My arms felt sore because I had been holding on to the grinder for dear life, and I realized I hadn't been breathing. I objectively knew that this sundering had taken less than a minute, but that was enough. My future had been sealed.

I guess a lot of people must have an experience like this and decide that maybe cutting through steel isn't for them. I sometimes ruminate, usually after I have cut or burnt my hand yet again, why that wasn't the case for me. I like to describe my younger self as angry. But what, you might ask, would I have to be angry about? I think that is the answer in and of itself. The suburban row houses I grew up in felt extremely safe. I spent all day, every day surrounded by objects designed to be used without being thought about. The entire environment, from the concrete slab of the footpath to the trimmed grass of the common green, all made me feel like I was being kept in a zoo. Like an elderly lady's pet cat: God's perfect killing machine reduced to pooping in a tray.

The angle grinder felt like escaping the zoo. Like the cat, after escaping the elderly lady's jungle of throw cushions, having a hair-raising encounter with a dog outside. I won't go as far as to say it made me feel alive, but it made me feel . . . more alive than I had been feeling. So, I was hooked on the feeling this tool, an electric motor with handles, gave me. With a motor that would pitilessly and messily unmake my meat if I lost my grip, it was like a much more grown-up version of the ones I played with as a child. I soon figured out that the 4½-inch grinder was much easier to use and provided more delicate results. These days, I use it as a one-handed tool and have the scars on my off hand to prove it (you normally hold the workpiece in your off hand, so it's the one that gets the abuse when abuse is being offered).

My next step was to learn how to weld. This was a trickier process. I don't think I did anything in art college that current me would call "welding," but I did find the "on" switch on a (stick) welder and occasionally would mess up two pieces of steel until they became a single, uglier piece of steel. The piles of molten slag I left behind would make anyone who actually knew how to weld weep. And I was one of the better welders there. Shuddersome. I remember being told I broke the MIG welder once and felt pretty bad about it. Either the technician wanted me to stop trying to weld so he could go back to reading his paper, or he literally knew nothing about welding. Either option is bad. The way I "broke" the MIG welder takes literally two seconds to fix if you are familiar with them at all. He put me back about a year in my progress. I stick welded so many things badly that I could have MIG welded badly (but faster) instead.

Now that I had access to some rudimentary steel-working tools, you can probably guess what the young guy with the long coat wanted to do. I think I was there less than three months when I started making swords. Or sword-like objects at least. It's odd. Young me still hadn't quite figured out that the crazy, impractical swords were much more to his liking than the efficient, historical ones. I think it was partially peer incomprehension. You tell someone you make swords, and if they start asking about anything at all, it will be about katanas and claymores and such. They ask about your anvil and your forge. There's a good chance they'll ask about pouring molten steel into a mold because movies have taught them to ask about that (you don't do that, even if you are making historical ones). They might start talking about a sword exhibition they went to in a museum. Who can blame them for trying to relate? It's better than the blank stares you'd get from most people.

Young me probably felt embarrassed to admit that his love of swords had much more to do with the PS1 than it did with history. I hope that in Universe B, where my YouTube channel never took off, I still have had the strength of character to not be self-conscious about that. C.S. Lewis had a quote that ran, "When I became a man, I put away childish things, including the fear of childishness and the desire to be very grown up." It still irks me a little bit when people call the opposite of what I make "real swords" as opposed to "historical swords." I know what they mean, but I sometimes have to suppress a little voice urging me to get them to explain what they mean. It doesn't matter what they mean. I know my swords are actual swords. It's just a shame there's no gorilla-strength super soldier hanging around who could actually use them.

The things I made back then were garbage, but if you squinted, you could sort of see what would become my aesthetic trying to break through. I got known as the guy who makes the swords, so that's what I did. The staff at the art college didn't like that. They pretty much hated everything I did there. Looking back at the difference between what they were trying to get me to do versus what I was actually doing, it is understandable, if insane. I'm probably the only person to pass through that place you've heard of (unless you are a fellow alumnus who decided to check this out because you know who I am, in which case, my point kind of stands, but also: Hello! Long time, no see!).

All told, I spent three years in that place. It would take current me about one week to teach past me everything he learned there in that time. Not that I'd do that. There are two reasons: One, I'd like to spend TWO weeks with him, so he could actually learn to do all those things properly. Two, I don't want to give you the impression that young me was continuously applying himself during those three years. That does a disservice to his comprehension ability. However, without the rigid prison-like structure of a Catholic boys' school, his work ethic, always shaky at best, basically dissolved in the face of having a peer group of society's edge cases to fraternize with. So, while I could teach him everything he learned there in one or two weeks, I might strangle him in the attempt, unable to tolerate (and secretly jealous of) his wanton indolence.

I think the most damaging thing any of the lecturers said to me during my time there was something along the lines of: "These are probably the best facilities you will ever have access to, so make sure to make use of them while you can." The facilities there were aggressively mediocre. But I didn't know enough to know that, which left me with a warped view of what was possible with hand tools. I left that place in 2003 with a barely passing grade, under the false impression that I'd never have access to angle grinders and a place to use them again. I was happy to be incredibly wrong.

CHAPTER 3

GOING UNDERGROUND: NITRIC ACID EVERYWHERE AND NOT A DROP TO DRINK

I GET A LOT OF EMAILS from people asking what equipment they need to start doing what I do. I will oblige with a little list if I have the time, but I often tell them the hardest obstacle they will encounter is actually finding a place they can work where others won't complain about the noise, fire, and sparks.

The thing about art school is it doesn't really leave you with any useful skills. So, after college, I was basically unemployable. I farted around for the summer and then started employment in a medical factory. Clean room environment. Harsh fluorescent lights. Medical scrubs everywhere. Beard net required. I fantasized about becoming a machine someday by having nanites slowly eat my brain and replace all the parts of it like the Ship of Theseus. The point of this fantasy was a kind of secular version of everlasting life, avoiding the decrepitude of old age. I felt the medical factory was also turning me into a machine, but in the opposite way: aging through repetition. There were thousands of component "A's" needing to get screwed into component "B's" every day, weird calluses developing on my hands, and lots of zoning out as a way of surviving. The young were selling their lives eight hours at a time making devices that helped the old survive. In winter, you entered the windowless clean room before the sun came up in the morning and left after the sun had gone down in the evening. Life was a blur of weekends. After the taste of the unstructured life I got in art college, it was a very difficult adjustment for me.

My plan was to try and establish my own workshop using the money I made from having a crushing adult job, but for various reasons that didn't work. My first attempt at a workshop was a classic garden shed, but that proved unworkable due to the risk of fire. I wish I had an anecdote about setting fire to a shed to share with you, but various nervous people made sure that I don't, and I was barred from trying to weld and grind in a civilian wooden shed. The shed features in the background of some of my very earliest videos, and it's still standing to this day, thanks to those nervous people. Clearly, I needed something made of concrete if I wanted to do actual work.

There are lessons to be learned about human psychology in almost everything. My father worked in a parking garage. It was built into a hill with half of the structure above ground, half below. People trying to escape it would descend this vast concrete spiral in their car and experience primal horror as they made the last turn and were not greeted, as they expected, with an exit, but with a concrete wall with a small door in it. The staff of the parking garage tried everything to get the humans used to the fact that the building's exit was midway up the structure and not at the bottom of it. But humans cannot follow even the most basic directions, and most of the staff's efforts only resulted in heightened horror. They switched off the lights on the lower levels. The thought was that descending into abyssal darkness would let the motorists who refused to read large signage KNOW they had made a mistake somewhere. This only increased the terror when they reached the pitch-black sump of the building.

If these unfortunate motorists were truly unlucky and descending into the bowels of the black spiral (circa 2004), they'd reach the bottom of the final circle only to notice that the small door in the unexpected concrete wall had weird blue light pouring out from beneath it. If they were incalculably unlucky, the door would open, revealing some sort of dungeon behind, and a stygian figure would proceed to shamble out and then up to their car.

I remember telling them, "You need to go up!" The now highly strung motorists would then ask me, in full seriousness and with a note of shrill hysteria creeping in, "WHICH WAY IS UP?" I pointed heavenward with my blackened finger, and they fled with squealing tires after making an awkward three-point turn.

Why this caused such panic in people was a little mysterious to me, but I can sort of see the shape of it if I concentrate. In the classic game *Silent Hill 2*, there's a sequence set in the bowels of a spooky subterranean prison where you proceed from section to section of the prison via irreversible jumps down into pits of indeterminate depth. It could have just as easily been stairs going down or a door on the same level, but the game wanted you to know you were descending, and there was no guarantee you were ever going to see the surface again. That really did an effective job of giving the player the creeps.

What I'm saying is, at the very bottom of that spooky prison in *Silent Hill 2*, you could find my first real workshop. The giant concrete spiral of the parking garage eventually met a flat foundation deep in the earth, and the ramp of the level above created a weird, wedge-shaped piece of waste space, so they walled it off. Thanks to the spiral, the entire structure had a light and air well down the center of it, and the light well opened up into that weird little wedge that felt like a brutalist Soviet version of an environment from *Alice in Wonderland*. So, not only was it an odd, unsettling liminal space, but it was also an odd, unsettling liminal space with a wet floor that smelled gross and had mosquitoes in the summer. The floor of the light well even collected random pieces of trash from the upper world like the bottom of the Mariana Trench.

It did have lights, and that meant it had electricity, so working by flashlight, I opened up the conduit and wired some electrical outlets in. If I were doing this now—and of course, I wouldn't do this now—the next step would have been to replace the breaker in the box with a larger one. I don't know what size breaker it was, but I was going to run a small welder off a breaker intended for a handful of fluorescent lights. It did not go well. I could weld for a minute or two before the switch tripped. In typical fashion, not knowing the actual solution, I developed a work-around. The breaker box was in the office where the security guards dwelled. I would work all day in the medical factory, which I cycled to and from, then I'd cycle to the parking garage and ask whoever was working if they wanted me to nip across the street to buy them smokes or whatever. In exchange, I asked them to flip the switch on the breaker if they heard it go click. They were all bored out of their skulls, so they were happy to oblige, but swapping the breaker out would have been a much smarter way to solve that problem.

Speaking of dumb solutions (ha, this is a pun because it was a chemical solution), it was during this time I first experimented with etching designs into steel. Toward the end of my time in art college, I discovered the printmaking department used nitric acid to burn plates for printing. I immediately wanted to try burning the designs into a blade and convinced one of the staff there to let me have some. I have no idea why printmakers use acids instead of a much less nasty method like electro etching, but my guess is tradition? I would not learn how to etch properly for another decade, but in that dimly lit grotto, I only had the advice of one printmaker to go by.

I'd use a roller to cover the steel in bitumen, and after it had dried, I'd scratch designs into the surface. Then I'd build plasticine walls up around the area I wanted to etch and come back a day later hoping for the best.

"The best" was always pretty crappy compared to what I actually wanted to happen. It was always a nightmare doing the cleanup. When I think of young, overtired me, using marigold gloves to protect myself as I sopped up nitric acid with a sponge and squeezed it into a bottle in my mosquito-filled dungeon, I shudder. I wish someone had explained to me that all I needed was salt water and a DC power supply; that it could be done in minutes, not overnight; and that I needed to get the designs printed out on a vinyl decal machine so I could relatively rapidly make copies and mirror images and such. I guess this was character building, but you don't need to damage your lungs with nitric fumes; use the saltwater method, please.

On the subject of doing everything in the hardest way possible, I had yet to discover Hardox®, so all these "swords" I was making were still made from regular "mild" steel, the softest steel you can get before it's just iron. It's the regular steel all structural components are made from, and it comes from the mill with a super thin layer of hard stuff called "mill scale" or just "scale." It forms when red-hot steel cools down while exposed to air. You can get aggressive acid to remove it, even just vinegar will remove it overnight, but I didn't know that. I didn't know a lot of things. So, I would laboriously hand sand these blanks for my swords (the angle grinder would leave too rough of a surface, because at this point, I didn't even know about sanding discs!). I would spend hours down there in the dark, sanding away amidst the mildewy stench.

I think the most depressing thing about this arrangement was the disparity I started to notice between how much work something was and the end result. I was developing valuable skills, chief among them the ability to stick with something and the knowledge of how much work making even the simplest thing from scratch is, but I was out to sea with the idea of placing a value on my work. I still am in a way. When you live in a world of mass-produced consumer products, you completely lose touch with how much effort it is to make ONE of something. That's not a criticism of people; by and large there's no need to know how much work making one of something is, but it did result in some funny exchanges with people early in my career, chiefly with myself in my own head. The market of mass-produced future landfill had anchored my own brain with the idea of how much something was worth, and because of the way I grew up, the art market of fancy custom-made objects was alien to me.

With the tools and skills I have now, I could knock out the garbage I made in my oubliette in a tenth of the time.

But these days, I wouldn't even like to put my name on the stuff I made back then. One of my best qualities is being real with myself and my work. I knew even then that the stuff I was making was terrible. I was selling my early work to people who had largely only ever bought mass-produced objects, AND selling it at a price that I MYSELF would buy it for, which meant I was hugely undercharging based on the man hours put into the work.

An awful trap aspiring creators fall into is an inability to see the difference between the amount of work they put into something and how much it would be worth to a third party. You see very funny amateur movies made this way. Chief among them is *The Room*. I have very strong feelings about Tommy Wiseau being hailed as a kind of folk hero for making the worst art. I think he typifies the problem of not being able to objectively view your own work and should not be dysfunctionally celebrated for it the way he is.

Even now, years later, everything I make tends to look bad to me: I can only see the mistakes. There's a small sweet spot where if I look at my previous project a few months later, it will look sort of okay, but everything before that and whatever I'm currently working on looks bad to me. I don't actually see this as a problem, but that might be because of the weird masochism of growing up in Catholic Ireland. I once made my therapist sad when she asked me if I knew what "negging" was. (For those of you who don't yet have a name for feeling bad after talking to a certain loved one, negging is when an actually awful person tries to convince you that YOU'RE AWFUL, and that you're really lucky that the actually awful person is willing to tolerate you despite the fact that you're "awful," otherwise you'd be completely alone.)

"Of course I know what negging is," I replied. I told her in traditional Catholicism you are taught that you are garbage, filth, the worst, but it's okay because despite the fact that you are the lowest form of sewage, God loves you anyway. I finished by explaining that now, as an atheist, I only believe the first part of that premise. She did not find it as funny as I hoped she would.

Years after that conversation, I moved to an island off the coast of Massachusetts called Martha's Vineyard and saw the problem of nonobjectivity about the quality of art on full display. The artists there live off the rich people who summer there, and these idle wealthy think it's cute to own art made by island-based artists. It's what's called a "codependent" relationship by people who study dysfunctional relationships. Retired wealthy people are poor art critics and generally buy landscapes and nautical-based knickknacks. This leads to a cycle where the artists there can't grow or do anything interesting and normalizes them producing the same art for twenty years in a row and overcharging for work that wouldn't sell outside of the island. Luckily, the local gerontocracy never showed an interest in giant comedy swords, so I was saved from this trap.

However, in the past, I was trying to come up with things I could make and sell. During art college, I was too distracted by the novelty of friends and a girlfriend, so my nerdy inclinations took a back seat for a few years. After art college, the girlfriend and most of the friends dissolved, so I found myself wanting to nerd again. I contacted the local university gaming group and became the creepy, off-putting older dude attending a college gathering. This led me to a bunch of gaming conventions in Ireland, and with that, I decided to make smaller stuff I could bring to conventions to sell. I never actually set up a booth or anything; I doubt I would have been allowed if I had asked, and besides, that would have cost money. I sold them out of my long leather coat like a video game's non-playable character (NPC), which was an aesthetic that, as you can imagine, the folks at these conventions liked quite a bit. My most popular item was these hair spike things I figured out how to make; nerd ladies with long hair loved them. It's a hair ornament you can potentially use to skewer a dude who's messing with you. The hair spikes led to one of my funnier dungeon mishaps.

At some point I realized I could put things other than drill bits into the chuck of the small bench drill I had and attack the things spinning in the drill with my angle grinder, iron files, sandpaper, and so forth. I can't remember the chain of thoughts that led to this revelation, but it would lead to a lifetime of using things that are not lathes as lathes.

The hair sticks (spikes really) were made from lengths of ¼-inch mild steel (that's about 6 mm in free-healthcare units). I'd start by carving the grooves on the end that would become the "handle," and then reverse it in the chuck and start tapering the other end down to make the spike portion. This involved a lot of hand sanding and filing, as well as angle grinding.

I always work with my hair tied up, but as anyone with long hair knows, if you work hard, random wisps will start to come undone. One night, as I stood there making a pile of these spikes, I got too close to the spinning apparatus. The loose wisps wrapped around the spinning chuck, which managed to grab more hair, which in turn grabbed even more hair. My rapidly accelerating forehead met the chuck with a painful clonk. Luckily, like all of my equipment, the bench drill was super cheap, so instead of ripping out a clump of hair, it started to slip on its drive belts. This resulted in me rapidly headbutting the chuck over and over again.

Bench drills generally have an emergency stop button on them. Big red button. Hard to miss. I will forgive the designers for not taking into account that a person's head might be glued to the drill, thus making it harder than usual to find the button. I started to flail like a fish, desperately looking for the off button while my head bashed off the chuck over and over again. I eventually did find the off button. I'm not sure how long it took, but it seemed to take longer than it should have. I was still entangled in the device and had to manually unwrap my hair from the spindle to free myself. No one knew I was down in that dungeon. I had a phone on me, but the reception was garbage deep underground, and I didn't have a single friend with a car. If I had been badly injured, I would have had to limp four stories up to the office with the security guard. Although most of the damage was to my head, which I clearly wasn't using anyway, I got lucky it wasn't too serious. All this to say: Keep your hair tied back when around spinning things, kids!

The piece of feedback I get most often is I should charge more for my swords, but that only works if you have the customer base lined up and they are anchored into thinking your product is actually worth money. Giant, silly fantasy swords are not quite in the art market; they tend to lean more toward the collectable market, and the collectable market is filled with mass-produced stuff. I think I was selling the hair sticks out of my coat for €5 a pair.

It was depressing to me that figuratively grinding away in the medical factory was so much more profitable than the actual grinding I was doing in my off time, so I developed a new plan. It only took me nine months of working in the clean room environment wearing a space suit to realize this life wasn't for me. I needed to work in a welding shop and have access to better . . . everything . . . than I currently had. I had already applied to a bunch of welding places and couldn't get a job in any of them based on my background as an art student. I did some research and found that Ireland had free adult education programs where you could learn actual welding/fabrication. The snag was they worked in six-month cycles. So, if I missed the opportunity, I'd have to wait six months for the next chance. If I quit my job, I would have to wait six weeks to apply for one of these programs, but if I got laid off, I could apply immediately. The next opportunity to join one of these courses began in a month.

I arranged a meeting with my HR person and asked to be laid off. They said they would think about it and get back to me. The clock began to tick. A week later, they told me they couldn't fire me. I said, "Okay," while thinking to myself, "How can I possibly win this game? I was trying to be nice." I needed to get fired. How can you not fire someone? I brought a cigar into the clean room and lit it up. I don't smoke, never have, but I took an experimental puff on the cigar just to see what it was like. It was so gross. I have no idea what the appeal is. I instantly started coughing and that's what made the line manager notice me and kick me out. I remember the HR person telling me, "This is not a good way to conduct your professional life. This incident will make it hard for you to get jobs in the future."

As part of my lonely, sad neckbeard lifestyle, I had read *The Art of War* by Sun Tzu (it's very short, which is probably why it's popular with the Roe Jogan mob). There's a quote in there that goes something like: "When your army has crossed the border, you should burn your boats and bridges, in order to make it clear to everybody that you have no hankering after home." I had no hankering to get another job in a clean room environment, but I didn't have a boat or bridge, so I burned a cigar instead. A burning boat would probably have smelled better.

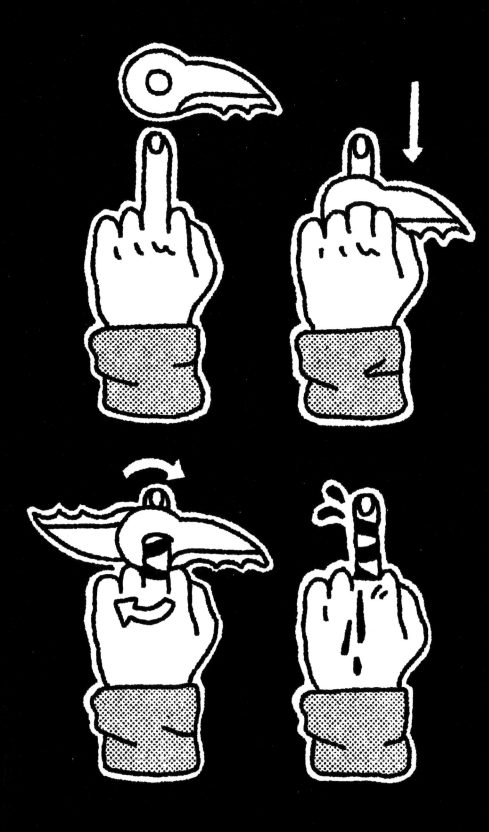

CHAPTER 4

FÁS AND
THE CUTTING
OF THE
BLOODY SPIRAL

FÁS IN IRELAND WAS AN ORGANIZATION that stood for Foras Áiseanna Saothair, which translates to something like "the help-you-get-a-job foundation." Colloquially, we joked that it stood for "Failed at School." It's called something else these days. It was an adult education program for unemployed people; if you were unemployed too long, you were told to take a FÁS course. You'd still get your unemployment money while on the course, but in theory, you'd be learning something at the same time.

This, of course, led to a lot of people who, after taking the courses, had no real intention of pursuing the trade in question. They were just looking for a way to stop the government from harassing them about not having a job for a while.

I think that's one of the reasons I got such a positive response from Jim Cleary, the guy teaching the course. All the teachers of the FÁS courses wore these white lab coat things that made them look slightly archaic. Jim had a friendly granddad vibe, which fits because I'm pretty sure he was a granddad by the time I was on the course. I know for a fact he's one now. A lot of the other guys on the course were looking at this as a speed bump on their path to what they actually wanted to be doing, but I had just come out of nine months of working in a clean room, so the welding course was the escape.

Just as I had been handed this amazing opportunity, however, I nearly messed it all up. My girlfriend from college and I were back together for a while. And then we weren't. And being a young man with the emotional bandwidth of a badly dubbed anime, I dealt with my resultant feelings by punching a wall. Unlike a Monster Energy Drink™ Kyle punching through some drywall, I made the mistake of punching an actual concrete wall. A couple of times actually, until one unfortunate hit exploded the metacarpal behind my right pinky finger. It wasn't the first or last bone I broke, but it was definitely the ouchiest.

I didn't actually know I had broken my hand until I tried using a hammer at FÁS the following Monday. Turns out it really hurts to hammer steel with a broken hand. I optimistically waited three days before finally admitting to myself that it wasn't getting better. At the hospital, they told me it probably wasn't broken because I'd be in more pain if it was and then they sent me for an X-ray. I guess going out with that lady had heightened my pain tolerance quite a bit because an hour later they were putting a cast on me.

When they were done, I had my index, middle finger, and thumb at my disposal on my right hand, and I still had a welding course to do. I knew I needed to prove that I could actually still do the course, otherwise I'd have to wait around for six months to catch the next one. So, the very next day, I cut open a welding glove and duct-taped it to my cast. One of the crucial features of a welding glove is that if it gets too hot, you can pull it off. I've had to do that a million times over the years, and I had just taped myself into one. I was worried an errant piece of molten steel would make its way inside my cast via the imperfect glove. Or that the heat would set the duct tape on fire. This didn't turn out as disastrous as I was dreading, and luckily the heat of the torch didn't seem to damage the cast. I did break the cast though. Twice. The first time, I went back and they slapped more material on top. The second time, I taped a thin steel plate I made directly to the break and called it a day.

I learned how to braze and gas weld with a broken hand. Even to this day, I will sometimes drape the oxyacetylene torch across my wrist in the position I learned to use while my hand had one too many pieces of bone. It takes the weight off your wrist and transfers the work to your bicep. Unlike the human heart, it only takes six weeks for bones to heal, and the welding course was six months long. So after the cast came off, there was still plenty of learning to do.

There were a million minor things I learned there that had been skipped over in art college. A center punch, for example. It's simply a length of hardened steel with a point, and you line it up where you want to drill a hole on a piece of steel and hit it with a hammer. This creates a little indent on the steel, and when you go to drill it, the tip of the drill finds the indent and you get the hole where you actually want the hole. I got through three years of art college, an art college that had a giant pedestal drill and drill bits, without anyone explaining to me that a center punch was a thing that existed and that it was something I should know about.

It was there that I discovered taps and dies, simple hand tools to put threads into a hole or on a bar of steel. I still use those all the time. I got to play with a press brake and steel rollers and an ironworker. I wish I could have started at the welding course in FÁS and THEN gone to art college, but alas.

One of the absolute best things, though, was all the practice I got doing actual welding. In art college, I learned how to turn the stick welder on and then awkwardly move the electrode around until the resultant mess was stuck together. Here I learned how to do actual welds where the molten slag would cool and then fall off by itself! The slag is actually the flux on a welding stick/rod; it protects the molten steel from the air, and then cools and hardens on the surface of the weld. If you weld properly, it should just fall off with the slimmest encouragement, but I'd never experienced that before.

One of my biggest revelations during the course though happened while I was using the MIG welder. Metal inert gas welding uses a gas, usually argon or a mix of argon and CO_2, as the flux, so the molten steel is protected from the air as it cools by a concentrated exhaust of fumes that don't react with the molten steel. Within moments of starting to weld with the MIG welder I "broke" it the same way I broke the MIG in college and had to suppress mild panic.

Instead of having a stick of flux-coated steel that melts as you use it, with MIG welding you have a spool of bare wire, which is fed to the torch via rollers that engage when you pull the trigger (which also unleashes the argon). Sometimes, if the welding hose is kinked, you spend too much time in one spot, or the speed of the rollers is set too low, the wire melts inside the nozzle to the copper tip of the torch instead of melting on the pieces of steel you are trying to join.

When this happened in art college, I was told I had broken the MIG welder, and it stayed that way for months. When it happened in FÁS, I was told to unscrew the gas nozzle and use a sanding disc on a grinder to remove the melted bit on the tip. After the two seconds it took to grind away the melted blob of steel, the wire, under tension in the torch, sprung out and was ready to use again. This whole process took less than a minute, and then I was back to practicing my MIG welding. All that stress over a nothing problem.

Of course, while I was there, I started making weapons, and poor old Jim Cleary didn't quite know what to do. I was clearly the person most excited to be there, but I was making sharp things. I'm sure the people who ran FÁS wouldn't be thrilled to know I was doing that. He turned a blind eye, but a blind eye that also wanted to see what I was up to.

An ironworker is a big hydraulic machine that concentrates all the things you might be able to do with a powerful hydraulic force into one heavy-ass apparatus. It can punch/notch/shear various sizes of steel. The part I was interested in was the punch. Putting a giant hole in a piece of steel was a huge pain in the butt for me before, but this thing could do it with a single press of a pedal, with "mild" steel that is. I still hadn't discovered Hardox; I don't know what would happen if you tried to punch a big hole through Hardox with an ironworker. My guess is the punch would explode, and if you got hit by the shrapnel, you would have a bad day.

I wanted to use the circular punch to bite a series of half circles out of a length of steel. I was trying to create a serrated "blade" with a series of teeth. As I stood there wrestling with the machine, it must have started making strange noises because Jimmy came over to see what I was doing. Having come from art college, I was expecting to be told to stop, as that was the feedback I usually got there. But once I explained what I was trying to do, he told me to tack weld two pieces of steel side by side at the ends, not to try and bite out half circles; it would be too abusive on the punch. He suggested I put the pieces through together and cut them apart afterwards to create two different pieces of serrated steel. Instead of telling me to stop, he offered helpful advice. This was the first time I'd ever experienced this. It seems like a small thing, but it was maybe the first time someone volunteered useful feedback to me about something that I wanted to accomplish, as opposed to begrudging half help in an effort to minimize my damage. So, I made two serrated swords instead of one.

The only dumb accident I had while at FÁS, broken hand not included, had to do with the ironworker and its ability to punch holes in things. I was making these small knife-type objects to bring to a nerdy game convention. I thought they'd look more interesting with a hole in the middle, so I took them over to the ironworker. After I sheared a hole through one, I thought it made it look like a punch dagger that could sit in your palm with your middle finger through the hole, so that if you made a fist, you could punch with the blade (I had not by then shaken all my neckbeard inclinations).

I slipped the knife on my middle finger like an oversized goth ring. I realized I had made a terrible mistake at around the same time that my inner monologue thought, "Huh, the hole is a little tight; I should make it bigger." The way the ironworker punches holes through regular steel is by squishing a round disc of hardened steel through the regular steel over a hole of the same corresponding size that's lined up perfectly. On the side where the disc gets squished into the steel, the edge of the hole is soft, almost beveled. This was the side I had inserted my finger. On the side where the hardened punch emerges through the regular steel, the edge of the hole is usually a jagged burr, especially on older punch sets.

Have you looked at the shape of a finger? There's a reason that rings tend to stay on. I gingerly started to twist the little knife off my finger, and the edge of the hole started to saw in. Mental images of the time I made the mistake of Googling "degloving" started to fill my mind. (Do not Google "degloving." I know you're tempted, but please don't.) I had a couple of options, but all of them involved using power tools right next to my finger and didn't seem particularly appealing.

At this point, one of the other guys on the course had spotted me and got curious as to what I was doing. I didn't want to gather an audience. I knew if I couldn't solve this quickly, there was a chance that someone might tell

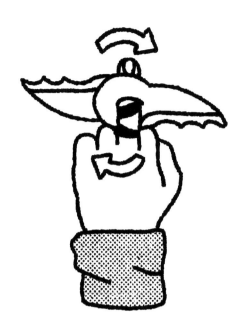

I GINGERLY STARTED TO
TWIST THE LITTLE KNIFE OFF
MY FINGER, AND THE EDGE OF
THE HOLE STARTED TO SAW
IN. MENTAL IMAGES OF THE
TIME I MADE THE MISTAKE
OF GOOGLING "DEGLOVING"
STARTED TO FILL MY MIND.

(DO NOT GOOGLE
"DEGLOVING." I KNOW
YOU'RE TEMPTED, BUT
PLEASE DON'T.)

Jimmy, and I didn't want to look stupid in front of him. To avoid that, I had to do something *really* stupid. I took a deep breath, closed my eyes, and began twisting.

Growing up, I was a big fan of the *Hellraiser* movies. When the remake came out, people complained about it as they always do, but like, have you seen the original *Hellraiser*? It's not a very good movie. And I say that as someone who loves that movie. As a teenager, I think what I responded to most was the weird pervy energy in that film. You take a film like *Halloween*, and there's this underlying subtext that sex will get you killed, but in *Hellraiser* it's not the subtext, it's the text. If you like weird pervy stuff too much, demons will come and take your skin off. It's ambiguous whether or not this is a reward or a punishment, but it often has the taste of the "victims" biting off more than they can chew. While most of the *Hellraiser* films feature people who inadvertently summon the Cenobites, their main prey is people who seek them out. This seemed like a more nuanced message than *Halloween* and the like, where the message is "sex bad, sex makes you dead." It's weird to talk about a film that features Cenobites tearing people apart with hooks as more nuanced.

This Clive Barker tangent has a point, I swear. Did you know that the phrase "exquisite pain" is an actual bona fide medical term? It SOUNDS like something Pinhead would say in *Hellraiser*, but no, it's legit doctor speak. It means "extremely intense, keen, sharp; said of pain or tenderness in a part." This was going through my head as I broke out into a cold sweat twisting this little lamprey mouth off my shredded digit. Don't stick your fingers in steel holes that seem NEARLY big enough! Especially if those holes have fresh jagged-ass edges!

When I opened my eyes and looked up, the guy who had originally noticed me was staring at me slack-jawed and slightly pale. I went to the bathroom and did the best I could with Band-Aid® adhesives and electrical tape. It was nowhere near a full degloving. (I'm serious: Don't Google "degloving!" If you already know what degloving is, you have my sympathies.) It was more like a bloody spiral that ran down the fattest part of my middle finger.

I went back and punched the holes out slightly bigger, and then sanded the edges of those holes before trying again (on my other hand this time). This time it slid on and off without any body horror occurring. These days, I probably would have made sure to punch the hole with plenty of room to spare.

My finest moment at FÁS was the time I made the breastplate. Through my connections with a street theater group called MACNAS, I was tasked with making a Roman-style breastplate for a play. Now, this was a prop for a play, so I could have made it out of the thinnest sheet steel possible, BUT I wanted to weld designs onto the surface, so I made it from stuff slightly over $^1/_{16}$ of an inch thick (or 2 mm in free-college units). I curved the plate in both directions with the rollers, cut out all the pieces I needed for the shoulder plates with shears (then rolled those too), and made hinges for the shoulders. I welded a big eagle inside a sun on the front and random laurels and squiggles onto the skirt. I never got feedback from the thespian it was destined for, whether it was too heavy for them or not. It was very heavy though.

When it was done, the FÁS people came and took photos of it. I have no idea what they used the pictures for, presumably to prove to people they were more than a service for warehousing time-wasters, but it put me in mind of making armor as a child. It was a thing the grown-ups could offer positive feedback about more so than the weapons.

Toward the end of my time at FÁS, there was a day when we could listen to a lecture about safety to get a card called a "Safe Pass." This would technically allow us to work on construction sites. It was during this lecture that I got the story about how angle grinders are extremely dangerous, as mentioned in Chapter Two. The crew who showed up to it were from all of the different FÁS courses: plumbing, carpentry, roofing, etc. At the end of it, the instructor came up to those of us who were from the welding course to expressly tell us there was no way to make what we do safe.

He explained that PPE is supposed to be a last resort, that standard safety protocol was to make it so that PPE was only brought to bear if something about the given operation went wrong. In welding/fabrication, the gloves, goggles, respirators, masks, aprons, etc. were all absolutely necessary because getting hit with sparks and eye-destroying light wasn't a mistake; it was standard operating procedure. I think he was trying to get us to second-guess our decision to become welder fabricators, but all young twenty-two-year-old me could think was: "Rad."

I did my welding exam and passed it, so I officially have a piece of paper somewhere that says I'm a bona fide welder. I am only sort of sure where it is. No one I have worked for has ever asked to see it. Times may be different now, but back in the first half of the 2000s in Ireland, no welding place actually cared whether you were qualified or not. Or at least, they didn't care about the piece of paper compared to your ability once you were actually working.

The very last part of the FÁS course was work experience. The deal was FÁS was still the one paying you during the work experience, so the companies in question were getting free labor. Like everything free though, those companies often got what they paid for, especially with the guys who didn't really want to be welders in the first place, so it had more of a babysitting vibe. Seeing as

I was of an artistic bent, Jimmy arranged for me to work at a place called Unique Designs, which did slightly more artsy stuff.

I think the shock of working there was because at FÁS I had felt somewhat competent for the first time in my life. All of a sudden, I was now working at a real welding place and quickly had to grapple with all of the things I didn't know yet. Like, I didn't yet know what it felt like to have powerful electricity flow through my body, or what it's like for your bare hand to fall onto a hot generator, but I was going to learn!

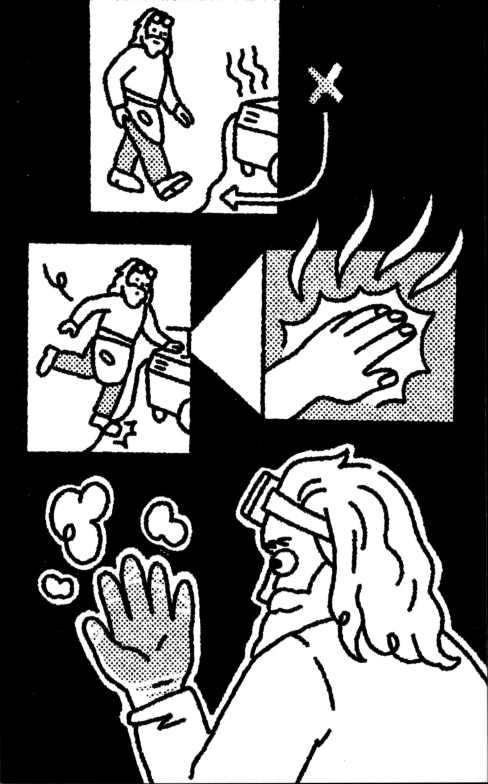

CHAPTER 5

PARASITE WORKSHOPS AND WELDING IN THE RAIN

I WAS TWENTY-TWO and had just finished training as a welder, but almost as soon as I got my first real job as a welder at a place called Unique Designs, I realized I wasn't up to snuff. There's a part in the film *Bringing Out the Dead* where Nicolas Cage, as a paramedic, says, "I realized that my training was useful in less than 10 percent of the calls." I felt like that a lot of the time. There are so many other skills involved with being a welder/fabricator than the actual welding and fabrication. The whole plan with doing the welding course was to get a job where I could use their facilities to make my own stuff on the side. Seeing as I was garbage, I knew I had to make myself attractive as an employee, so I offered to work for the same amount as the Irish dole money (unemployment). It's what I was getting while doing the welding course, so I'd already figured out how to live comfortably on it. The fact that I didn't drink made the money go further.

BUT I wanted to work part-time, only three days a week, and have access to the workshop after hours. The boss, Padraig, agreed, and that was the arrangement for the next couple of years. The main lesson I learned at Unique Designs was the ability to make a weld completely disappear. In FÁS, we were mainly learning how to stick stuff together so it wouldn't fall apart, and not so concerned about the cleanup. At Unique Designs, I was introduced to the flat sanding disc, which if used carefully, could completely hide a weld between two pieces of steel.

There's a meme in welding that if you need to grind a weld, you're a garbage welder. This stems from a misunderstanding about the purpose of a weld. If you are just trying to do a structural weld for the purposes of making two pieces of steel stick together, then grinding the weld might serve no purpose other than hiding the fact that your weld was messy and gross. I've never really understood this thinking because if a weld is messy and gross, you'll still be able to tell after you grind it. A bad weld will be full of porosity and so forth, and grinding the weld will only bring all that nastiness to the surface more and make it easier to see. During my welding test, they chopped my weld in two to see a side profile and see if there was any porosity. If my weld had been full of little bubbles, I would have failed the test, but it was solid all the way through, like a weld should be.

At Unique Designs, we made fire escapes and so forth where there was no need to grind the welds, but we also made decorative gates, furniture, and fancy spiral staircases. Even a good MIG weld will be kind of lumpy, so we ground everything and blended everything together so there was not a single spot on it where a person could catch their hand on an uneven surface. This wasn't "bad welding." Even in industrial applications, there are plenty of instances when you would need two parts you've welded together to fit against a third component smoothly.

In my sword work, I started to use this approach to weld everything fully and blend things, while also using welds as decorative elements in other instances. It was here that I discovered ready-made finials and such for use in gates and rails and started to incorporate them into my swords. I don't do that much anymore, but if I need a 4-inch steel sphere for something, I know you can just buy those off the rack.

I had lots of minor cuts and burns while working there (I say minor, but I have a pretty big scar on the back of my right thumb from one, so maybe I should say "pedestrian" injuries), but there were a few incidents that led to me questioning my brain's ability to brain.

We were out on-site somewhere doing . . . something . . . I can't remember what. There was no power at the place, so we were using a mobile generator. Everything was going fine until toward the end when I tripped over one of my welding cables "umbilicalling" from the genny. In an effort to save myself, my bare, ungloved hand instinctually found the top of the generator and all of my weight was momentarily supported via my bare palm on the engine's top surface. It turns out the top of a generator gets pretty hot.

In the classic home invasion fantasy *Home Alone*, there's a part where Joe Pesci grabs a red-hot doorknob, only to have the "M" of the McCallisters' custom knob branded into his palm. Before my hand fell onto the generator, I had always doubted how accurate this scene was, as the M is delineated quite finely, and my guess had always been that with seared flesh, surely the fine detail would be lost amidst all the blistering and charring. I no longer doubt. I spent at least a week with the sharp ninety-degree corner of some plate from the top of the generator sharply marked on my hand. You could even make out the shape of three of the Phillips-head screws that held the plate down, clearly enough that you would have been able to fetch the right-sized screwdriver to undo those screws by looking at my palm. Don't touch the top of generators!

It wasn't always super hot things though; sometimes it was really cold stuff that got you. On a rainy occasion, we were at the front of a building welding some I-beams together for a big new front entrance they were building. I was up on a ladder, and it was raining hard, and I was thoroughly soaked, and that's when I learned a new way to get hurt. So, the way welding works, in case I haven't mentioned it, is you make a circuit; you connect an earth or ground to the piece you want to weld, and when you touch the torch off the steel, the circuit is complete and the steel melts in a controlled fashion.

Outdoors is too windy for MIG welding; the gas gets blown away and you're left with messy welds, so it's mostly stick. The problem with stick welding is you can't continuously do it or you'll melt the stick, and then need to load another one. This is normally fine, but if everything is wet, I mean really soaked, I discovered the end of the stick will be able to complete the circuit through your drenched body. I did a funny little dance at the top of the ladder as the current passed through me, but I got the new stick loaded. AND THEN I KEPT GOING. I'm too old for that nonsense now, but I stayed up on the ladder, getting zapped every time I used a stick up. I eventually figured out that you could sort of get the stick into the mouth of the torch by throwing it like a dart. You may be wondering why I didn't turn the welder off between sticks, but like I said, I was at the top of a ladder. In order to do that, I'd have to climb all the way down every time. No one has time for that. I think if I was doing it now, I'd maybe have kept a plastic bag inside my coat to grab the new sticks with. Or I would just refuse to weld in the rain. But that's kind of a hard sell in Ireland. Don't weld in the rain!

I still wasn't wearing a respirator at this stage. It was a relatively late addition to my gear because, honestly, none of the other welders I saw wore them. One of the worst activities to do while NOT wearing a respirator was working in the painting booth. I don't know how much paint dust I inhaled, but luckily, I had a second accident while cleaning out the paint gun, so it's probably fine now; to clean out the paint gun, you loaded it up with thinners and blew that through the gun. Also while wearing no respirator. One day, while cleaning the gun out, I lost my grip after filling the tank up with thinners. I flailed my hands out trying to grab the gun to stop it from hitting the ground, and I succeeded! I grabbed the gun, and the trigger (!), midair, while it was facing directly toward me. I shot a huge gout of paint thinner directly into my eyes and open mouth! What I'm saying is, you might have been concerned about all the paint dust I inhaled, but I also inhaled a huge amount of thinner, and in the ensuing hacking coughs and attempts to wash my eyes out, I'm pretty sure I thinned out and then coughed up a massive amount of the paint that had solidified in my lungs. Health! I wear a respirator these days, and so should you.

It was while at Unique Designs that I made my first Buster Sword. Do I have to explain what a Buster Sword is? Is there any chance you bought my book and don't know? I guess I should give a brief explanation. *Final Fantasy VII (FFVII)* was an extremely popular video game in 1997. Like I mentioned before, Ireland came into money in the '90s, and a huge proportion of kids had PlayStations. The only country where the proportion was higher was Japan. It's weird to think of how much of a mania *FFVII* caused; it's a JRPG—or Japanese role-playing game, basically an interactive book—but had *Dungeons & Dragons* (D&D) elements like leveling up and buying equipment for your characters. And it was long. The longest game any kid in Ireland would have seen up until then. It seemed like every kid played it. The main character is a waspy young male with spiky yellow hair, inexplicably called Cloud Strife, and his main feature is that he is armed with ENOR-MOUS swords. Comically enormous. Imagine putting a handle on a surfboard enormous. It was the coolest thing any young lad in Ireland had ever seen. It definitely went into my head and did permanent damage. The sword he starts the game with is called a "Buster Sword," and much like the one I was about to make, it's the worst sword in the entire game.

Thinking back, it's strange that it took me so long to get around to making one. If I had to guess why, and this is just a guess, I think I was still struggling with the idea that swords are supposed to be usable. I wasn't fully comfortable with the idea of them as purely art objects yet; I still had a little fedora and trench coat left inside of me that I needed to shed. These days, I've carved out a very specific niche for myself, so most people don't get confused, but you still come across this tension every so often. Guys will send me emails asking if I can make them a historical Viking axe or whatever, as if you can't get those anywhere.

I can't even remember the name of the guy who asked me to make the Buster Sword. He was a friend of a friend. I also don't remember where I got the measurements, but I know I made it too big. I think the total length was 2000 mm, or for Americans, 1 Michael Jordan long. The blade was 300 mm wide, which is ironically longer than Michael Jordan's foot but is about a foot wide. Luckily for me, the Buster Sword is an incredibly simple sword in design, a big rectangle with an angle cut at the top and two holes in the blade near the guard. I still messed the design all up; I was not yet very good at this.

The main hurdle with the blade was polishing it. I hadn't yet discovered removing mill scale with vinegar, and the scale was slightly too hard and smooth for the sanding discs I had. I very carefully and gently broke up the surface with a regular grinding disc before going over it with sanding discs. Don't do this. No matter how gentle you think you can be, the grinding disc will leave nasty marks that will take way too much effort to clean up. Also, I don't think I had the discipline to keep the sanding discs moving in the same direction, as I got impatient with certain areas that had deeper grinder disc gouges. There's nothing worse than the random swirly marks from undisciplined grinder work. I think I tried to hand sand it afterwards, but at that point, I had done too much damage to the blank. It was a mess.

Polishing a giant slab of steel is still a daunting task, but these days I have an actual method. I usually start with the vinegar bath: I'll use a big rubber sheet and some bricks or whatever to create a bath big enough for the slab and leave it soaking in vinegar overnight. I think because the mill scale is so thin, and barely actual steel (mostly oxides and such), it dissolves in the vinegar overnight. After that, I'll use a sanding disc to very gently remove the surface texture of the slab; the key here is keep the sanding disc as flat to the surface as possible without applying any pressure and to move in even, smooth lines. Next, a regular belt sander with a succession of belts of different grits is used, and if you are very lucky, you can get a surface with no noticeable gouges or dings. I usually only polish my giant blades to 100 grit, I find that any grit higher than that becomes very difficult to maintain on the giant blades.

Someday, when I am rich from book sales or similar, I will purchase a huge machine known as a stroke sander. A stroke sander is basically a gigantic belt sander, designed for the exact purpose of polishing great big slabs. I could go straight from the vinegar bath to the stroke sander. They aren't actually that expensive, but I'd need to be rich to have the space to keep one; it would be the biggest tool I'd own.

These days I make my handles out of solid stock, but I couldn't find anything big enough at Unique Designs. I made a weird Frankenstein thing by welding the biggest solid bar I could find inside not one but TWO hollow pipes. The way I welded it to the blade was questionable, but I'm sure I did my best given the circumstances. One of the reasons I use solid bar these days is you can bevel the entire depth of the bar and weld from the center of it out to create a join that's 100 percent weld.

Weirdly, Unique Designs didn't have a plasma cutter. When I was in art college, I remember they only had one auto-darkening welding helmet; it was kept under lock and key, and we weren't allowed to use it. On a rare occasion when the technician was actually present, he told me the helmet cost £300. These days you can get much better ones for $40, and I'm sure they are considered basically disposable, going by how hard it is to fix them when they break. I wonder if plasma cutters went through a similar price drop in the decade and a half since I made the first Buster Sword…

Plasma cutting involves creating an arc of superheated ionized air through your workpiece, and then using that arc to cut through it with electricity and compressed air. When I have to make a hole through something like a Buster Sword these days, I'll start with the plasma cutter to get it as close as I can, and then clean the hole (or whatever shape) up using a die grinder, an electric iron file type gadget. I have mine mounted sticking up through a flat table, so the sides of the hole would be a clean ninety degrees after.

At Unique Designs, I didn't have a plasma cutter OR a die grinder, so I improvised. I used the oxyacetylene torch to make very crude holes where I needed them, then welded in pipe sections where the nice round holes needed to be. The pipe sections were fatter than the base plate, so afterwards, when I ground down the weld, the remaining piece was actually round. This further messed up the surface in those spots despite my best efforts.

When I had finished making it, I knew something special had happened, as ugly as the result was. Normally when I finished making a sword, I'd take my 3-megapixel digital camera and take a picture before the sword disappeared to whoever it was for. Then I'd print out that picture on my Inkjet™ printer and place it in a clear envelope in a ring binder folder I called my portfolio. I can't remember, but I don't think the camera even had an SD card. Once that computer crashed, the shitty Inkjet pictures were the only record of the sword existing at all other than the physical copy that existed somewhere in the world.

Earlier that year, I'd started uploading videos to YouTube sporadically. It started because some of the things I was making had moving parts, and a crappy Inkjet printout wasn't quite able to capture the objects in motion properly. With the Buster Sword, I found the pictures weren't quite able to capture how silly the sheer size of it was. It needed a video.

A friend of mine called Podge helped me film the fateful video. He was the one who introduced me to YouTube in the first place. The video we made was awful. Truly terrible. It's unwatchable these days due to it being in 240p, the finest "p" that 2007 could offer. You can't understand if you weren't there; we'd use our Nintendo Wii to sit and watch anime uploaded in ten-minute segments in 240p for HOURS. Playlists were clunky, so we had the chance to realize we were wasting our lives every ten minutes and instead would keep watching. Even if it had been filmed in glorious 4k, it'd be an awful video; it's too long and uses cringey music, which makes what happened next extra inexplicable.

I'm not a fan of *Dungeons & Dragons*, so when I say D&D, I mean the whole class of tabletop role-playing games (TTRPGs) where players fight monsters to level up and get imaginary gold to buy imaginary weapons, rinse and repeat. *FFVII* was that sort of game in digital format, except it came with stunning visuals for the time and a prewritten story that people found intriguing, and there was no "role-playing" required on the part of the player. I think the part of TTRPGs that makes them intriguing is the amateur theater aspect; they give you a chance to inhabit a character you create.

Gary Gygax, the creator of D&D, was a wargamer; his background was in games where you pushed armies of miniature soldiers across a battlefield and resolved esoteric game mechanics to figure out which army is winning. When he decided he wanted to make a sort of *Lord of the Rings* simulator, he used what he knew, and D&D was, and still is, mechanically mostly a tactical combat game.

These days you can get the tactical combat itch scratched by any number of video games, but you can't get the role-play itch scratched by anything other than games like D&D. Since D&D, many other TTRPG have emerged that lean into the role-playing part and eschew the complicated rules for small-scale combat. What I'm saying is, as unpopular an opinion as it may be, TTRPGs were such an appealing concept that they survived and thrived despite the first iteration of the idea being literally the worst version.

I sometimes fantasize about a universe where Gary Gygax was a theater nerd who liked fantasy stuff and a dash of math. I don't know how many potential role-players the hobby loses each year to the ponderous rulebook of *Dungeons & Dragons*. They probably walk away thinking, "Gosh, those kids on *Stranger Things* sure made this look a lot more fun than it is!" Those people who will never learn about the instant fun of *Tales from the Loop*, *Star Crossed*, *Magical Kitties Save the Day*, or a million other games where the core of the fun (collaborative storytelling and amateur theater) isn't paywalled behind reading hundreds of pages of rules for various combat situations.

I sometimes think of this when I remember that first giant sword video, how garbage it was, and what happened next. The idea was so appealing to people that it survived its first and worst version. I'm lucky in a way that the video was only in 240p; it covered up my poor craftsmanship. I sometimes joke that my ability to make things look nice has kept pace with the video quality available on YouTube, and I'm only half joking. Despite all my hard work up until that point, I still think what happened next was the purest form of dumb luck.

CHAPTER 6

AMERICA! (AND BOILING MY FACE OFF)

THE YEAR 2007 was pretty crazy for me. The video of me swinging the Buster Sword around went live on September 22nd. It got twelve views in its first twenty-four hours of being live. On November 29th of the same year, my daughter was born. During my bachelor days, I would save up money and go traveling, then come back and save up money to do it again. I spent three months in New Zealand and a few weeks in various European places. I went to New Zealand to see *Lord of the Rings* stuff. I went to America in February of 2007 to see H.P. Lovecraft's grave. That didn't take very long, so I went and looked at New York and Boston and so forth. At a nerd convention in Boston, I met the woman who is now my ex-wife. We lasted fifteen years together, which isn't bad for two strangers who were kind of randomly thrust together.

I left Unique Designs at the end of September to go to America and be part of the birth of my kid. When I returned in January of 2008 for a visit, I got stuck in Ireland. Apparently if you have an American kid but aren't yourself an American citizen, you get labeled as a "high-risk Visa jumper," and they can deny you entry. Of course, you can get around this by getting married to an American citizen, so my ex-wife and I were married by April of 2008.

But before that could happen, I had to get a job and such in Ireland. The first of many "Once in a Lifetime" recessions had just started, so Unique Designs couldn't hire me again, even in our weird arrangement where they paid me next to nothing. I got a full-time welding job at a different, much larger place called Rynn Engineering. The problem with Rynn's is that it was more professional, so they were not cool with me coming in after hours to work on my own projects. I did anyway, but I had to be very sneaky. It's hard to be sneaky with swords as big as surfboards, so my progress slowed.

This lasted for about a year, during which my popularity on YouTube was small but gaining some traction. Having uploaded a video of myself failing to use a comically unusable sword, I almost instantly started getting messages from fellow weirdos who also wanted the opportunity to not be able to use a humongous sword. However, trying to work a full-time job while also being a new dad, making swords on the side, and trying to keep my social life going took a toll on my physical and mental health. The problem was most of my audience was in America, thanks to the nature of the interwebs, but I secretly suspect that even if Americans hadn't been dominating the English-speaking webdernet, the giant silly unusable swords would still have been most popular in the land of the Humvee.

In 2009, I decided I wanted to move to America to be near the market for giant swords. My ex-wife's family had land on the island of Martha's Vineyard, and a local artist there called Barney Zeitz wanted me to work for him part-time, similar to the arrangement from Unique Designs. There was an old unused building on the property I could convert into a workshop. It seemed like the perfect answer. To top everything off, in October of 2009 the comedy website Cracked featured the Buster Sword video. On the day the video was uploaded, it got twelve views. On the day the Cracked listicle went live, it got an extra 24k views. I just went and double-checked that; I can't believe that was such a big deal at the time—24k seems like nothing these days. My most popular video on YouTube now has 11M views. But apparently 24k views was enough to cause my inbox to explode. Other nerdy websites started noticing my videos too, and the snowball rolling down the hill started getting bigger and bigger.

One of the cool things about the Vineyard is I had no social life for the first six years I was trapped there. I could have been busy every night if I was into acoustic potlucks and organic guitars, but as a nerdy guy who believed vaccines worked? I was extremely lonely. H.P. Lovecraft was an awful human being in quite a lot of ways (the main one being his racism), but one of his better qualities, also borne of loneliness I suspect, was his insistence on answering every single piece of fan mail sent to him. I decided to emulate this approach, and I still try to do it to this day. There's no way to do the math, but I really believe this helped develop the channel in the early days.

Either way, it was made possible through a combination of being trapped on the Isle of Solitude and only having a part-time job. On the subject of the part-time job, I learned some incredibly important stuff working with Barney, techniques I still use to this day. The most important of which was to not be shy with the grinder.

Unique Designs was a welding shop with arty leanings, but Barney is an actual artist. This means he charges art prices for his pieces, so he can afford to spend time on techniques that just aren't feasible in the normal-people market. Barney would take these huge chunks of steel and go to town on them with the 9-inch grinder: giant solid bars would become these delicate spiraled pieces. I had already learned at Unique Designs about making a weld disappear, but from Barney, I also learned you can build up a crazy amount of material between two shapes before you start grinding. The amount of material he laid down was almost like 3D printing, and then he'd grind back to get these incredibly organic shapes that looked more like castings than the result of welding and fabrication. Animals. Insects. Even human faces he built up this way. When I've used this technique, it's mostly been for skulls. Skulls feature prominently on many giant swords. This insane amount of grinding, and Barney's insistence, were the precipitating circumstances that led me to start wearing a respirator in earnest at all times.

I had learned brazing with a broken hand while at FÁS. It's normally used as an alternative to welding for smaller or more delicate joints, or joints between non-steel or dissimilar metals. The brazing rod is usually made of brass or some other alloy with a low melting point. While I had seen the potential of using brazing as a technique to inlay brass into grooves on steel, I hadn't considered it as a method for completely brass coating an object. Barney would braze the entire surface of a chandelier or sculpture. This creates a rough, organic melted type of surface texture that makes the result look like something archeological. There's another technique for brass coating an object: You simply heat up a piece of steel and hit it with a brass brush. The brass is soft and transfers to the surface of the warm steel. The advantage of this approach is you don't lose any surface detail on your finished piece. The disadvantage is same as the reason why you don't lose any detail; the brass coating is incredibly thin and will come off with any sort of abrasion. It's also kind of a muddy-yellow color as opposed to the bright look of polished brass. Using the Barney approach of brazing an entire surface, you're left with a brass coating so thick you can literally polish it up with a steel wire brush mounted in an angle grinder, and while kind of rough, it can be buffed to an incredible luster. There's no other plating technique that leaves a surface this thick on your finished piece, even if you splash out and send it to a fancy plating place. I liked it because my swords were expected to take abuse, and this is the strongest technique I've ever found other than making the piece out of a giant piece of brass in the first place (and depending on the sword design, using an actual giant lump of brass would sometimes lead to a weaker sword more prone to breaking anyway).

The funniest accident I had at Barney's involved rediscovering the principles of steam power. I can't remember why I was heating up the end of the pipe, but I was heating it up and hitting it with the hammer to shape it for some purpose. When I was finished, I dunked the pipe in a bucket of cold water. But it was a pipe. A pipe that was red-hot at one end, dunked into water. I inadvertently had made a device for shooting steam and boiling water at my face. I know the end of the film *Total Recall* is supposed to be happening inside Arnold Schwarzenegger's head as his brain dissolves or whatever, but one of the things that always bugged me as a kid was the climax. Spoiler alert for a film nearly old enough to serve as a U.S. president I guess: An alien machine melts the icy core of Mars and clouds of atmosphere boil out of Pyramid Mountain, "saving" the day. The boiling clouds are violent enough to shatter all the glass hab domes on Mars, and the bewildered inhabitants all marvel at the new blue sky and breathable atmosphere. Surely all the inhabitants of Mars should have been cooked to death? Something something alien technology, I guess. Also, it was all a hallucination anyway. A steam burn is apparently a worse species of burn than regular boiling water because not only does the steam raise the temperature of your face to boiling water temps, but it also releases the energy it inherited turning from a liquid into a vapor as it condenses on whatever surface it's scalding. Surfaces like my face. Luckily, I closed my eyes, so they were fine, but I had a weird scaldy-looking mug for a while. Don't stick the ends of red-hot pipes into water! Or at the very least, angle the end away from yourself!

I can't remember exactly WHEN I discovered that vinegar can be used to strip rust and scale from steel, but I remember the WHY. There are a lot of swords that are various interesting colors in video games and so forth. A lot of the interesting bright colors you can only achieve using paint, which will scrape off with use. I hate paint, but there are some colors that you can get to stay. I've already mentioned the brazing that leaves a gold color. You can also braze with silicon bronze for all the shades copper can turn. You can in THEORY treat either with acid for verdigris; that's a green. Of course, there are the orange and browns of rust. Heat, while not delivering a very thick or strong surface, can leave oxides that are gold or blue or purple, and while it's not very thick, it looks better than paint. I even made a sword with all the colors of the pride flag once (I was nervous about calling the video "Mike's Big Gay Sword" as opposed to "The Pride Sword," but many of my gay-quaintances said it was fine). Then there's black. There are a lot of swords that are black in various angry young-man fiction.

You can buy a chemical for "cold bluing" steel, aka turning it black. The black is an oxide that's just a type of fancy, more stable rust. For whatever reason, I was suspicious of the cold bluing solution, and sure enough, the sample piece I tested turned rusty. The cold bluing solution is a type of acid, and if you don't rinse the piece thoroughly, it can make the piece regular rusty again. Of course, if you don't dry all the water you used to rinse the piece off with thoroughly, that will rust the piece too. And then if you don't oil the piece afterwards, that will also cause it to start rusting. So, there are a few failure points, and when I did my first experiment I must have hit one of them because it was years before I attempted the cold bluing solution again and discovered it worked fine.

For the moment though, I tried other experiments. The most successful I found was letting a piece of steel get super rusty and then boiling it. The problem is a fresh coat of rust is actually super loose on the surface, so while I had some luck using hydrogen peroxide and vinegar to rust steel quickly, this process could still take days to make the steel turn a species of gray instead. It's a tough coating, stronger than the cold bluing true black, but you have to be very generous to see it as black.

On some knife-making forum somewhere, I found a guy who mentioned he used boiling vinegar to make his knife turn black. I have found you always have to take info from forums with a grain of salt. Forums attract a weird crowd, and the weirder the person, the more time they'll have for posting on forums. I have seen sword guys advise each other to only quench in rainwater, others to align their quench buckets with magnetic north so their blades won't warp when they dunk them. Others advise that organic canola oil is better than the cheap stuff for your quench bucket. Boiling vinegar seemed like a low-investment experiment to attempt, so I decided to give it a go. I wanted to see the difference between applying this technique to bare steel vs. mill scale, as the mill scale itself is quite a tough surface if you can keep it intact, and if you could reliably make it turn black, it might be interesting.

I set up a pot to boil and threw the steel sample in (Pro tip: Don't boil vinegar indoors; it's stinky AND stings to inhale). When I took it out a few minutes later I was disappointed; it initially did look black, but as I rinsed it off in the sink all the black disappeared. Not only had the polished piece of the sample not blackened at all, but it had taken on a matte appearance as the vinegar had etched it a bit. Furthermore, because the vinegar was hot, the surface began to flash rust almost immediately before I rinsed it off and dried it. But then I noticed the side I'd left the scale on. The scale rubbed off with just my fingers. Not quite believing what I was seeing, I rinsed it under the faucet and sure enough all the scale was gone.

If you haven't spent years grinding the tough outer layer off large steel slabs, it's hard to articulate how important this was. I had wasted so many abrasives trying to remove the mill scale without damaging the plate underneath. Of all the methods I have discovered on my channel over the years, absolutely none have been as useful to other people as this, based on my inbox. Unlike nitric acid, which regular people can't buy, or muriatic acid, which regular people shouldn't buy, vinegar is so safe that lunatic fringe people on Martha's Vineyard drink it instead of getting their flu shots. You can use it to clean the scale off of fresh steel, but also the rust off of old steel. And you can pour the resultant soup on the ground afterwards without feeling too bad. As for the nitric acid of dubious origin I used up: I can't quite remember how I got rid of it, but it involved doing something shady, like breaking back into the print department there after hours and pouring it into their hazardous disposal jungle juice drum.

I mentioned I started wearing a respirator when I was working at Barney's. At FÁS, the uniform was a set of blue overalls, but by the time I was leaving there I had switched back to just my leather apron. At Unique Designs, I got away with wearing whatever I felt like, aka the apron. I also started wearing the distinctive shoes with the metatarsal plates while there, but I never really wore a respirator. They are uncomfortable and no one else was wearing them. Earmuffs also weren't very in vogue there, despite all the racket of the grinders. Safety glasses and gloves seemed acceptable, but the safety glasses were communal, and it was always a struggle to find a pair that wasn't scratched up. At Rynn Engineering, the official uniform went back to being a set of blue overalls, and there it was a more rigid company policy. I wore my apron over the overalls sometimes if I was doing a lot of grinding, but I think all the Polish guys smoking cigs while welding and grinding would have laughed at me if I wore a respirator. A lot of the older guys in there had faces so weathered they looked like they had survived GRU assassination attempts. Nope. Not Novichok. Just the life of a welder.

Seeing as I was now living more of the life I actually wanted at Barney's and could do whatever I felt like, I started to experiment more with my PPE. I was still wearing the more traditional type of respirator, the type you see on my logo, with the cans and so forth that lock directly to your face with the straps. There were many reasons it was difficult for this to become part of my standard kit. The first was the safety glasses. Whatever shape my head is, the standard safety glasses fog up on me when I wear a normal respirator. I solved this by discovering the older type of safety goggles while working at Barney's, the type that have been completely co-opted by steampunk enthusiasts. It is now easier and cheaper to buy a pack of five of them painted in steampunk colors than it is to find one that is intended for actual work with sparks. I also find it's slightly harder for sparks to get around the edge of them than the edges of traditional glasses. Barney was an earmuff enthusiast, so I started wearing those too.

Between the 1400s and 1600s in Germany there was mercenary group called Landsknechts. They were famous for flamboyant outfits made from random scraps of brightly colored stuff they pillaged from the battlefield. These dudes looked FABULOUS. There's some quote I can't find now, someone asking some king was he not embarrassed to have all his fighting done by a heavily armed Psycho Pride Parade, and the King or Count or whatever responded by saying something like, "Their lives are short and brutish and usually end in them having their insides turned into outsides; if looking like a circus tent makes them happy, what kind of monster would I be to take that away from them?"

With that in mind, and because of the goggles probably, I spray-painted and modified my respirator, goggles, and earmuffs to look steampunky. My apron was by then a giant mishmash of patches, and if I needed additional protection in some location, I was usually liable to strap some random extra plate of steel to myself in a modular fashion. I was starting to look pretty nutty, but I wasn't quite done.

Because of my beard, I had to strap on the respirator extremely tightly to get a good seal, and because I wore braces as a kid, when I'd take it off in the evening, I'd have to wait a half hour before my teeth would fit together properly again. Also, when polishing steel, sometimes a big glob of my spit would fall out of the exit valve, necessitating me cleaning up the flash rusted spot from my acidic sputum. I also didn't like the way the straps tangled and caught on my beard and hair.

A friend of mine introduced me to the "Resp-o-rator," an alternate contraption for guys with beards. You put it in your mouth like a snorkel and wear a nose clip. Pipes that rested on your shoulders connected to filters at the back. I had to modify mine a bit, so I steampunked that too, and behold! My look was complete. I've heard people refer to me as a "steampunk fantasy dwarf," which isn't a terrible characterization. A weirdo who makes giant swords in the woods while wearing 1980s fingerless leather gloves, a shirt with a bunch of holes in it, an apron made of a mass of patches, a weird steampunk scuba contraption with a baby bottle glued to it, and earmuffs with a pressure gauge glued to the side would be more precise.

I'll sometimes get emails from guys who have modified their own PPE to look weird or have fabricated up respirators like my one. Other than the vinegar trick, my other great contribution to my little corner of culture might be making PPE a fun thing instead of an unmanly hassle that interferes with your ability to suck on cancer sticks.

As for my videos, while still nowhere near the quality they would eventually get to, I had started experimenting with setting everything on fire. Living in the woods away from row houses and cities, I learned I was a late-blooming pyromaniac. I filled plastic bags with propane to create fireballs; I filled coconuts with gas to make Molotov cocktails (I didn't want to get glass on the ground). I set random stuff on fire in the background. The first time I filled a pumpkin with gasoline and hit it with a sword, I was bare chested (Video: Sword of Omens, Amerikaner Edition). I survived unscathed somehow. Madness.

Other people were starting to notice the madness I was up to, and eventually they came a-knocking.

CHAPTER 7

THE ROAD
TO
HOLLYWEIRD

THE YEAR WAS 2012, and I had just finished making a sword called Rebellion from the game *Devil May Cry*. It was a long, relatively skinny sword with a blade a mere 4 inches wide (skinny as these giant ones go). It was mainly notable for having a guard that looked like a rib cage with a skull, the handle and crossbars looking vaguely boney. My ex-wife was doing a story for the local paper about an NPR event happening on the island. In attendance was going to be a guy called Steve Junker. He did little segments for NPR called *Creative Life*, where he'd interview local people about what they did on "the Cape and Islands." She wanted to know if I'd like her to hassle Steve Junker to do a segment about me. I said, "Yeah, sure, why not?" Though I doubted he'd go for it since I wasn't very "Cape and Islands." I'd heard some of those segments, and they were always about an elderly fisherman or a guy who seduces clams or whatever. They always ran about the same way:

Steve: "Tell us what you do."

Elderly Man with Stephen King Accent (EMWSKA): "Well see, first I get the clams, see."

Steve: "Uh huh."

\<Indistinct bucket-rattling sounds\>

EMWSKA: "And then . . . Then I fill up the bucket with the clams."

\<Sensual moist shellfish sounds\>

Steve: "Yes."

EMWSKA: "Then I drop my drawers."

Steve: "Oh my god!"

Well, my ex-wife went to the NPR event, cornered Steve Junker there, and he said, "Yes, please, 100 percent! I am sick of doing stories about oyster fanciers." Lesson? Never assume someone doing something is doing it by choice!

The segment about me was called "Giant Swords and Little Movies." It aired in January of 2013 and can still be found on the Internet to this day. He did an AUDIO recording of me smashing a pallet with a giant sword. I thought it was fun but didn't really expect anyone to care. Well, it turns out a lot of people listen to NPR in the den of liberal darkness known as New England. I was already known in the bubble of Internet weirdos and listicles and forums and such, but that story got me locally known. Thin, nervous WASPs (White Anglo-Saxon Protestants) who can't play video games because they're afraid of the gluten in them all of a sudden knew who I was.

Now that I'd breached out of my Internet-only bubble, the following summer a nice pair of guys called Eric and Jason from the *Cape Cod Times* showed up. They made a short video for the newspaper's YouTube channel called "The Man Who Makes Giant Swords." The video was disproportionately popular compared to the others on their page, and again I reached a bunch of people who hadn't previously known I existed. I was, and still am, quite happy in my little echo chamber of nerds who like swords and video games, but apparently the almighty algorithm who sorts us by our shopping preferences had been keeping people in Hollywood from seeing me. I am convinced that someone from LA was holidaying on the Cape that summer and came across the video, then I rode in their head like a memetic virus back to the City of Angels.

I didn't just receive one email about the possibility of doing a TV show, but several emails, from different people, all within the same short span of a couple of months. My default assumption about the Internet trying to offer you an opportunity is that a scam of some sort is afoot. The thing was, I couldn't figure out what the angle was with the TV show bit. This just shows how naive I was. These days, my paranoid brain would have assumed the ruse involved the production company getting me to sign a contract that gave them exclusive rights to do a TV show with me, and then hold onto those rights on the off chance that someone ELSE wanted to do a TV show with me in the future. Then they'd force the other production company or even me myself to buy them out of the contract. Amazingly though, my suspicions turned out to be unfounded (on this occasion).

They didn't make me sign anything. They wanted to talk to me, presumably to see how much of the personality on display in my videos I could summon on command. Unbelievably to some people, there's not much of a difference between the me you see in my videos and the me you meet in real life. It's more of a distillation than an exaggeration. The next step was they physically sent someone from the production company to check me out in person. I think this may have been one of the few ways being on the Vineyard helped me compared to being in some much cheaper, anonymous part of America. I can imagine the conversation they had about coming out to meet me:

Boss: "Hey, do you want to go on a business trip to fancy-rich-people island to talk to a guy about doing a show?"

Interviewer: "Damn straight, I do!"

For a total of three times, someone came out from LA to talk to me: one from the production company, and then two from Discovery Channel. I showed them what I did and my world, and little by little, it became more likely that they were going to do a show. A little note in case this is not clear to everyone, "production companies" make the shows, but the "networks," like Discovery, are the ones who fund the making of the shows. Production companies are always pitching show ideas to different networks. The network's goal is to figure out if they can make more money selling the real estate in the ad-break slots than they spent making the thing in the first place.

The Discovery network decided to proceed, and I instantly got knots in my stomach. The working title of the show was "Big F'ing Swords," then later changed to "Big Giant Swords" when they chickened out. The very late change in name, without consulting me, initially made me disproportionately angry, and I responded by purchasing biggiantswords.com and using it to host a gif of me playing Jenga® in the nude with my willy. I think my outsized reaction was the result of months of no one consulting me about any creative decision to do with the show, a show they still expected me to promote as "my own." The new name did eventually grow on me, like my willy, but I still own biggiantswords.com to this day.

There were many disagreements over the show's artistic direction. Given complete control, I would have wanted the show to be something like Bob Ross but with swords. They wanted it to be more like every other reality show at the time. That meant they had to assemble a team of people who "worked" for me. The fiction of the show was to be that I had quit all of my other work completely and was assembling a team and my own business and so forth. In real life, this is incredibly uncharacteristic of me. I believe in taking little baby steps to minimize risk, which is still why only a small number of people know who I am, but I've been around for nearly fifteen years on YouTube with no sign of stopping when the average lifespan of a YouTuber is about five years.

One of the first things we clashed over creatively was the origin of the swords being so giant. The reason a lot of my swords are huge is because they are replicas of video game weapons. This is probably as good of a place as any to talk about discovering Hardox. I was using regular steel for most of my weapons, occasionally stainless, as I had deemed that good enough for the big giant silly swords. I had decided at some point that the "giant" part of what I do was less important to me than the "weird" element, and that I could make smaller weapons too, as long as they were eccentric in some way. So, I got commissioned to make a regular-sized sword that I deemed weird enough to interest me and, by extension, my audience. The only problem was I didn't want to make it out of mild steel. For normal-sized swords, regular steel is just way too soft. I had made some smaller ones out of spring steel, aka old leaf springs from the backs of trucks, and I had even made a weird one out of a giant old band-saw blade. This new commission of mine was just a little too wide to use any leaf spring I could find. I'm not sure which one of my million pieces of correspondence mentioned "Hardox," but I decided to look into it. It's a type of plate steel that comes already hardened and tempered. They use it for the

"GIVEN COMPLETE CONTROL,
I WOULD HAVE WANTED THE
SHOW TO BE SOMETHING LIKE
BOB ROSS BUT WITH SWORDS."

scoops on diggers, the beds of rock loaders, and anything else that has to take a bunch of abuse. It's not as good as the steel they use for "real" swords, but you can get it cut to literally any size. I decided to order some and was extremely impressed by it. It's nearly impossible to drill a hole in it and, unlike the leaf springs, it can take a weld without any sort of preheating or weirdness. Testing it by hitting the edge of a ¼-inch piece of Hardox against a piece of ¼-inch mild steel, the Hardox took huge gouges out of the mild steel without taking any damage itself. Since discovering it, I haven't used mild steel to make a sword.

I bring up the decision to make smaller weapons too because it relates to the show and the Brobdingnagian proportions of the weapons on it. The production company wanted to drop the video game replica aspect entirely. With the video game element dropped, the reason the swords were so huge became obscure. If they had told me it was because they didn't want to deal with the licensing issues associated with depicting weapons from trademarked properties, I could have respected that. Instead, they maintained that the video game aspect would alienate a large portion of the audience, as only children played video games. This is not true in 2023, and I highly doubt it was true in 2014. The statistics showed that only 24 percent of people who played video games in 2022 were below the age of eighteen, with the average gamer age of thirty-five. It's getting pretty close to any given fact about the average gamer being the same as any given fact about the average person. To be fair to them, this might not be true of regular TV-watching audiences, who skew older, but they specifically told me one of the reasons Discovery wanted the show in the first place was to attract a younger audience.

So, they wanted me to pretend I had a team of people helping me and wanted to drop the video-game-replica aspect, but surely they'd still keep the aspect where I poured a lot of care and detail into my creations? The premise of the show was to be that I had to make one giant weapon a week. Oh, and a smaller weapon too while I was at it. That would be the B plot. I started to get stressed out, but I rolled up my sleeves and got to work as best I could. The weapons were to be prepared in various stages of completion ahead of time early in the summer of 2014. Most of the filming was to happen during a six-week block late in the same summer.

One of the people we assembled to pretend to be my team was AmeriMike, a fellow beardo who did nerd games. He sometimes helped me film my YouTube videos, so we were going to pretend he was my constant cameraman. Erik, AmeriMike's friend since school, also liked nerd games but had an interest in making swords and such, so we pretended he was my assistant in the shop. He did actually help me get the half-finished swords ready. A talent scout also recruited Jamie, a lady blacksmith that I saw around at artisan shows and such on the island, and Jonny, who lived up the road from me, but whom I had never met before filming. Finally, the local charter school had a mentorship program, and I had volunteered for it, so there was a kid called Matthew who had been coming to my workshop every Wednesday for a couple of years. I convinced them to include him too. In reality, Matthew had spent more time in my workshop than any of the others.

Erik and Jamie helped me as much as they could prior to filming, but there was still a massive amount to be done on the fly when the crew showed up to actually film. A few of them told me afterwards that they'd never worked on a show before where the main star of a show had to work through the night during the actual production and that something had gone wrong organizationally. It was like the island was punishing me for trying to make a trashy reality TV show on it. They initially promised to hire other guys to help work on the swords while I slept, but seeing how the island is, the other welders/fabricators never materialized, so I didn't sleep. On top of that, there were constant struggles about what the episodes were going to be about and such.

Here's a secret: Reality TV exists as a union-busting technique. You hire actors who aren't actors and writers who aren't writers, make them sign crappy contracts, and then you don't have to pay anyone royalties. If the show flops, it didn't cost you much to make, but if the show is a success, then boom! You rake in a bunch of money without having to share any of it. Reality TV has an outsized presence on the airwaves compared to its popularity for this very reason. For a few years after they made the show, I'd get excited emails from a slew of French people or Germans telling me they liked the show. They paid me for the six episodes we did, but like most reality TV "stars," I haven't made a penny from them airing the show anywhere since. I got them to buy me a big pedestal drill, my own oxyacetylene rig, and a plasma cutter that I still have, so there's that, I guess.

I'm still super glad I did the show, as stressful as it was; it helped get my name out there and finally convinced me that I could do the sword stuff full-time (which, ironically, was the fictional premise of the show). I still didn't have enough money to hire help after the show, but I did have enough interest in me to make it my own full-time job.

With this crazy, helter-skelter schedule, you'd think there would have been more accidents on set, but I only suffered one injury on the show, and it didn't even involve the giant flamethrower sword. I'd wanted to make a *flammenwerfer schwert* for a while, but I couldn't get anyone to commission it and was kind of worried about all the ways it could go wrong. Luckily, the show was created back to front compared to how I normally did things. I came up with the sword idea, and they found the customers afterwards. The swords were often based on previous things I had made that they wanted me to try making again in episode format. For example, the episode "The Destroyer" was based on a sword I had made called the Sumida Sword, "Zeus Almighty" was based on a sword I made in my video "When Idiots Fight with Electrified Swords," and the episode "The Junkyard Crasher" was based on my video "Atrox the Junk Sword vs. Car."

I could stretch a little. I had wanted to make a sword for Sarah Robles, Olympic weightlifter, for a while, ever since I had read a story about how she had to drive herself to tryouts and sleep in her car and such, but I couldn't find a gap where I could pass up paid work to do a freebie sword amidst all the commissions that I was falling behind on. So, when the show came up, I had an opportunity to get Hollywood to fund that project and get Sarah a little extra exposure. A few years later, she brought home the first Olympic Weightlifting medal America had won in sixteen years.

The show also presented the perfect opportunity to create the flamethrower sword that I couldn't get any of my real customers to go for. It was a giant sword that looked like a huge dragon's head and shot a huge gout of fire supplied by a propane tank that I wore on my back. I didn't die. It was great. Wait. Why was I . . . Oh yeah, the one injury I got . . .

My wrist started to hurt really bad during filming, worse than anything before. In my regular life, I'd make a giant sword, which would take a month or two (oh boy, it takes so much longer now, but more on that later), and then I'd swing it at a target and have a sore back for a little while afterwards, maybe a stiff shoulder. With the insane production schedule of the summer, I'd been working around the clock to get everything ready, and it still wasn't ready by the time shooting started. The shooting schedule was six weeks, so I had to work through the night on more than one occasion. There were six episodes, six giant swords, and I was swinging those giant fellas at stuff at least once a week. I strained the tendons in my right wrist and couldn't grip stuff. Doc said it was tennis elbow from playing tennis with the world's biggest rackets. They gave me pills and wrapped up my wrist in bandages, but the show had to go on! I was in quite a lot of pain through the last half of the production, which probably didn't help my mood. If any of you guys involved with the show are reading this: Sorry I was grumpy.

The show aired in the first part of 2015. I don't watch reality TV, so I don't know what makes reality TV good, but I was told it was good as reality TV goes? Unfortunately, it left the regular reality TV–watching demographic a little cold, and eventually they declined to renew. They were hoping for about a million viewers per episode, and it consistently fell slightly short of the target. The highlight for me was when William Shatner live-tweeted that he was watching an episode. The episode featured Matthew getting his own leather apron for outstanding contributions, and Captain Kirk watched and cheered along; it was surreal.

After the show, there was a huge influx of messages on the Michaelcthulhu Facebook page and my regular inbox. Like I said, I was finally convinced that I could turn the sword stuff into my full-time job, so I did. The weird part was noticing how the TV–watching world and the Internet are two nonoverlapping bubbles. There was a small uptick in my view numbers while my show was on, but it was nowhere near the amount I got when a nerdy website did a feature about me. I felt there was something in the air about me that I needed to capitalize on but could sense it was already starting to fade away. I realized I couldn't rely on a moderately popular reality TV show to stabilize my popularity; I needed to grab the reins.

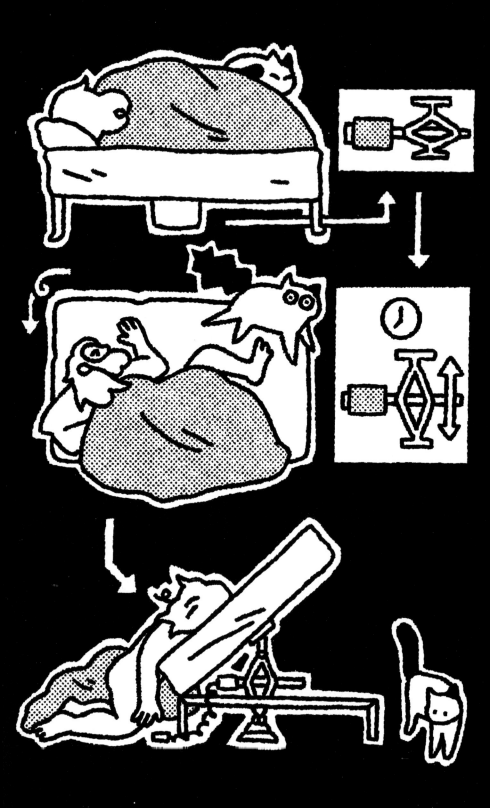

CHAPTER 8

PATREON: A MILLION STEEL SPLINTERS IN MY SKIN

I HAVE ALWAYS BEEN a casual fan of heavy metal, especially the faster, louder subsets of it. Death. Thrash. Synth. One of the advantages metal has over the gentler genres is if you are working with headphones on, you can actually hear it over the sound of the angle grinders you are using. I like to think the channel, with the giant swords and fire and destruction and so forth, has always lived up to having a heavy-metal aesthetic to match the actual heavy metals that I work with. I tried to squeeze as much of this as I could into the episode of the TV show called "Hell's Hound," where I created a sword called Cerberus that splits into three. The production crew found a band called "Hound of Hades" to play the part of the customers, which was pretty perfect.

In the 1889 book *The Golden Bough*, James Frazer coined the term "sympathetic magic." You'd ritualistically imitate some outcome you wanted to achieve in the hopes of making it more likely to occur. Part of the theory was that ancient peoples were painting successful hunts on the sides of caves as a way of increasing the chances of the hunt going well. Same idea with voodoo dolls. It's a similar species of weirdness to what can be found in *The Secret*. Athletes are asked to visualize their successes before they happen. I don't believe in any sort of supernatural stuff myself, but if I did, you couldn't have asked for a larger, more elaborate ritual than the episode with Cerberus to summon Erik Lindmark out of the aether.

Erik, RIP, was the founder of Unique Leader Records and the lead guitarist for Deeds of Flesh (Do I need to tell you that Deeds of Flesh is a metal band? You figured that out through context clues, right?). The mascot of Unique Leader is a sick-ass horned demon called Alrekr, with three eyes and a rotting face. Erik wanted me to make a sword where the guard was formed of Alrekr's head and horns. Of course, I jumped at the opportunity. The show had just recently ended, and I decided that instead of complaining that the show wasn't in the format I wanted, I could just make the show I wanted and post that to YouTube. So, I decided to give the "Bob Ross with Swords" experiment a go.

In retrospect, I should have been doing this years and years before I did, but there were some fairly stupid misunderstandings holding me back. Whenever I watch a YouTube video about how to make or fix something, it's because I want to make or fix a thing. A lot of solutions to do with welding/grinding are pretty obvious to me already, so I tend not to watch those kinds of videos. I was, and still am, way more likely to watch a video about fixing a dryer or whatever (because I wanted to fix my dryer). For YouTube entertainment myself, I'll watch a compilation of people falling down, some science edutainment, or a deep dive into some niche Internet mystery.

For years I had been receiving emails from people asking me to post videos explaining how to make their own giant swords. I resisted strongly, theorizing that the video would be useless to anyone without access to a full welder/fabricator shop, and everything in it would be too obvious to someone who did work as a welder/fabricator.

I caved in late 2013, and in January of 2014, a full year before the show aired, I released "How a Buster Sword is Built." During its first month of being live, it received 13k views and generated a whopping $17. I felt vindicated. People seemed to like the video, but the amount of time and effort it took to produce it was staggering compared to the shorter videos of me smashing stuff to heavy metal music. It wasn't until months after it was uploaded that I noticed the trend. While the shorter videos usually got a very intense burst of views once they went live, this tended to quickly taper down to nothing until a website would feature the video in an article about me. The thirty-eight-minute Buster Sword video bucked this trend, chugging away in a steady trickle. By the time a year had elapsed and the TV show was wrapping up, the build video had amassed 633k views and had generated about 900 bucks. Now, the amount of effort it took to make the video was still far in excess of 900 bucks, so it was still

"DO I NEED TO KNOW HOW A FLUORESCENT TUBE IS MADE? NO. WOULD I LIKE TO SPEND FORTY MINUTES WATCHING MACHINES MAKE ONE? YES."

a failed experiment by that metric, but I could sort of see the shape of things to come in it.

I liked Erik and Unique Leader, so I thought it might be good to produce something that would attract similar customers. The Buster Sword video proved I was wrong about the popularity of "how-to" videos being linked to their utility. I would have realized that if I had remembered the appeal that led to hours of me watching *How It's Made*. Do I need to know how a fluorescent tube is made? No. Would I like to spend forty minutes watching machines make one? Yes. I decided to start filming every step of making the Alrekr sword.

My major technical innovation with Alrekr was that I had purchased a pencil grinder. The electric die grinder I had been using was large and clunky. I had set up the table for it, so I could use it to carve the edges of plates at ninety degrees delicately, but it was still too difficult to hold and perform delicate work with. A pencil grinder is like a Dremel®. The one I bought was air powered to make it even slimmer. I could hold it like a chonky sharpie. The ¼-inch carbide heads are like little iron files that spin. The face of Alrekr is all rotten flesh. Using layered plates and the pencil grinder, I achieved a level of detail higher than any of my previous swords, including teeth inside a jaw peeking out between strips of ruined cheek.

Very soon after getting the pencil grinder, I discovered the little steel splinters it leaves. It's still my least favorite of all the workshop-related danger dander. An angle grinder throws off a spark; the spark is a tiny piece of hot steel igniting as the ratio between its surface area, temperature, and available oxygen collide. Grinder dust is nasty stuff too, but the biggest risk to life and limb it poses is inhaling it. The regular-sized die grinder, being more like a spinning electric file, throws off little shards of steel instead of sparks. They're bigger, and not quite hot enough to ignite (most of the time). I'm not sure why, but they also tend to be magnetized. I've noticed the Hardox plate tends to be slightly magnetic, so maybe it passes that on to the shards being thrown off it. Being magnetic they tend to stand up and out on steel surfaces, so as your bare hand brushes across a surface, they are all aligned like little pikemen, ready to bravely impale the monstrous being bearing down on them. The tiniest steel splinter has a way of making its presence felt in the most acute fashion. These days I carry a splinter kit in a tiny tin case with me everywhere, which consists of a pair of X-Acto® blades for digging and a pair of tiny tweezers for grabbing (in pairs, in case I drop one).

The pencil grinder makes splinters that are even smaller and more delicate than the regular die grinder. With the full-sized die grinder, I could usually wear gloves while using it, because the work was not super fine. I had specifically gotten the pencil grinder for the purpose of doing delicate work. I'd learned it was the side of my hand (the part you karate chop with when you need to fight ninjas) and the heel of my hand (the part of your palm you use to drive a thug's nose back into his brain while defending your pregnant wife outside a bar in Mobile, Alabama, triggering a chain of events that leads you to helping retake control of a plane full of convicts that has been hijacked by John Malkovich) that tended to get the worst of the splinters, so I taped those up with duct tape. It sort of worked? Since I've started using the regular die grinder and the pencil grinder more and more, it's basically become lethal to casually pick up anything in the workshop. Every tool needs to be looked at and, because of the magnetism, usually tapped off the side of a surface hard before you can trust holding it in your bare hand.

Once Alrekr was finished, I started the laborious task of editing all the footage together. I asked Erik, since this sword was basically a promo for Unique Leader Records, if I could have some tracks to go along with the visuals of me making the swords. This started a long relationship with a second guitarist in Deeds of Flesh Craig Peters, which is still going strong to this day.

For the testing of the sword, I made and wore huge metal wings. Cardboard inserts set into the wings and set on fire assured that I looked like a Balrog while swinging the blade at various targets, which were also on fire.

The video went live and got about 100k views in its first month, at about $1 per 1,000 views, so it made about $100 during that first month in Google AdSense. People seemed to really like the video, but it still wasn't quite financially viable to spend my time filming every step of making a sword and then editing the result together.

Patreon is a "support the artist" type website. You sign up to give your favorite artist some money every month, Patreon takes a chunk and handles the logistics, and the artist gets a deposit into their account, no fuss no muss. I'd been avoiding it for a bunch of reasons. I think the main one was confidence. I knew people liked my stuff, but that didn't mean I liked my stuff, and it seemed weird to me to set up this "support the artist" type of thing. It seemed like begging. The psychological hump that made me get over it was thinking of the long videos as a product I was making that needed to be paid for, just like the swords themselves. The video of me announcing I was starting a Patreon is still up there, and I think you can tell that I'm kind of embarrassed to be asking. I hate when artists hide their content behind a paywall, so I intended to upload the build videos one way or another, and AT MOST, the videos of me making the swords would only have a delayed release, not be locked up indefinitely, so really there was no need at all for a patient person to sponsor me.

I had realized early on that not everyone could afford a giant sword, and that while the Google AdSense money from YouTube was neat, it was super unreliable. To that end, I had tried setting up passive income with my T-shirts and miniature 3D-printed versions of my swords: "Hey! If you give me a SMALL amount of money, I will send you this thing!" Both had only lackluster results. I was incredibly surprised when the Patreon took off like a rocket. "Hey, give me a small amount of money for NO REASON IN PARTICULAR!" turned out to be the absolute BEST passive income source. Explain that one, economists!

Now, before all of you rush out to set up your Patreon accounts, I have a word of advice. I had been making YouTube videos for eight years AND had been on American national TV before attempting the Patreon thing. Like a lot of the things in my life, I could have probably set up that account a few years before I actually did, but I couldn't have set it up in 2007 after uploading the very first Buster Sword video and gotten the same results (Patreon didn't exist until 2013, but that's not the point I'm making). Also, yes, my therapist is talking to me about my confidence. It might seem weird to have to talk to a guy who basically runs an international cult of personality about his lack of confidence, but there you go.

Patreon was founded by Jack Conte, one-half of the music duo Pomplamoose. He's a pleasant hipster-type dude, but like a lot of friendly hipster musicians, he smiles way too much and I suspect doesn't know how to handle anything negative very well. I've attended "Creator Live Streams" for people like me on Patreon. I have no idea if these still happen, but my guess is not. He'd invite some local artist friend of his to join him, "This is Jemily who does little paintings using paper straws and paint and a spinning paper disc . . ." and everything would be super chill. A running chat on the side invited people who have made Patreon accounts to ask questions, and here the "problem" of Patreon is laid bare. Jack obviously wanted to talk about the creative process, Patreon's features, etc., but in the running chat at the side there is only one question: "How do I get more people to sign up for my Patreon?" Jack is too nice to answer this question.

Sometimes my Vineyard artist friends would ask me about Patreon because hearing me describe it would inspire them to want one too. I get emails from young men who want to copy my model and set up a sword-making Patreon and want advice. I tell them both the same thing: Without already having a following, there is no real point. You have to focus on building up a following FIRST. There is probably no harm in setting up a Patreon early, but don't expect it to do a single thing until you have a large following. I have a million subscribers on YouTube these days, and of those, only a thousand sponsor me on Patreon. That's a 0.1 percent conversion rate, and it's pretty good as these things go. The danger of Patreon is people growing disheartened by thinking it's a shortcut to making a living from your art. There's no shortcut. All Patreon ensures is that there's at least a finish line. That's more than you're promised in general by trying to make a career doing something creative.

Back to my moderate success. It seemed like I had landed on the winning formula. The cost of filming myself and then editing together the long videos was covered by Patreon, so the YouTube money almost didn't matter. Better yet, a strange synergy started to occur. Once I started uploading long-build videos on the regular, my view numbers started to climb, almost to the point where I COULD rely on the Google AdSense, until the Ad-pocalypse occurred at least. At my peak, Google was sending me about $3,000 a month, which got halved over a few short months and never really recovered. The short version is: YouTube got greedy about what kinds of videos it would allow ads on. I remember getting an email from YouTube pre-2010 congratulating me for qualifying for advertisements on my great videos. I don't know when, but at some point shortly after that they stopped the policy of only allowing established creators into the adshare program.

They switched to EVERYONE being able to put ads on their videos as soon as they created an account, with zero oversight. This allowed journalists in 2017 to take screencaps of ads for Coca-Cola® and baby food playing beside beheading videos, anti-Semitic discussions, super niche fetish material, and so on. In response to public outcry, many advertisers pulled out of YouTube. This caused YouTube to overcorrect, making it harder than it ever was before to qualify for ads on your video. So now you can spend months making a video only to have it "demonetized" (barred from having ads) because you said the word "assist" at some point and the algorithm thought it heard you say "ass" or whatever. The future is dumb and getting dumber all the time. Using the Patreon money, I could experiment with longer, more elaborate builds. Every commission went extremely over budget, but that was fine. Putting more detail into the swords resulted in more elaborate videos, which my fan base liked, generating more income. I could send swords out to get professional coatings like black oxide or expensive and delicate brass coatings. I had an extremely complicated head for a mace called Sunkeeper professionally (robot arm) plasma cut through 1-inch-thick Hardox. I shudder to think how much time it would have taken me to make the shape by hand. I have no idea how much getting it robo-cut cost. The cost didn't matter. I purchased a TIG welder.

Outside of a handful of sloppy TIG welds while working at Rynn's, I'd never been trained how to TIG weld,
but I had learned to broken-handedly gas weld a million
years ago in FÁS. Gas welding is one of the most primitive
forms of welding, and the type that Hollywood usually
shows when it has to portray a welder. You use an oxyacetylene torch to heat the steel to melting and introduce a
rod of extra material that melts into the gap, and when
it all cools, you have a join. It's slow, the workpiece gets
extremely hot, and it works best on thin material. When
people ask me what kind of welding class they should
take, I always tell them to make sure the class includes
at least stick welding but also MIG, as a course that only
teaches gas welding is kind of obsolete.

IRONICALLY, it turns out the technique you use for
gas welding is very similar to TIG welding, which is one
of the cleanest, tidiest ways of joining steel together.
Laser welding rigs have begun appearing in the home
market, but for the moment, TIG welding is the best
welding you can get in a home workshop. TIG stands for
Tungsten inert gas. Unlike the stick welding, where the
electrical arc melting the steel is provided by the tip of
the stick making contact with the workpiece and melting
it into place, and MIG welding, where a constantly fed
wire is the thing that provides the arc and the welding
material, in TIG welding, all the torch provides is the

arc and the gas to shield the arc from the air. A tungsten electrode, like an old-fashioned arc light, is tough enough to withstand the temperature involved in maintaining a constant arc. You hover this just over the surface of your material, making it molten at the point where the arc makes contact, while introducing a stick of material into this molten pool from the side with your other hand. The tricky part, unlike gas welding, is to avoid making physical contact between the rip of the tungsten electrode and the thing you are trying to weld, or the electrode and the stick of material you are introducing from the side. We're talking a few scant millimeters of a gap here. If the tungsten electrode gets molten steel on it, it becomes very difficult very quickly to maintain a nice clean arc, so you have to take it out, resharpen it, and try again. I'm still not a great TIG welder, but a mediocre user of a TIG welder can still achieve tidier and more delicate joins than a skilled user with a MIG or stick welder.

After the first year on Patreon, I noticed a problem. It would be a few years before I would be formally diagnosed with ADHD, so all I knew was I had to make constant deals with myself in order to get anything done. In any situation where my willpower was involved, I endeavored to remove it as a factor. In a failed attempt to get me to go to bed earlier, I sealed a timer switch inside a box and connected it to my house's Internet router. The timer was set to kill the Internet between two and four in the morning. When that wasn't good enough, I built a device from a ½-inch impact driver, a scissor jack, another timer switch, an emergency stop switch, and the most frightening wiring you ever saw for tilting my entire bed at forty-five degrees at ten every morning (It's featured in the video called "Mike's Alarming Bed," which was on Canadian National Television). As well as throwing me out of the bed, it made a horrifying racket. I stopped using it the morning I woke up at noon in a kneeling position in front of my tilted bed (see illustration on page 127).

To this end, I set up my Patreon so that I only got a payout from the people who signed up once I actually uploaded a video. The idea was that this would incentivize me to get a video done every month. When I was doing the TV show, I was putting out one sword per week, so I thought that I should be able to do one per month easy peasy. What I didn't take into account was that a lot of those swords I made on the show were already half finished, and of course someone else was doing the filming and editing. But surely without the constant interruptions to film reaction shots and talking-head bits, it would be faster? I also didn't take into account how much time was "wasted" each day answering emails and babysitting social media posts. The first year of Patreon, I generally did a lot of simpler swords and just about managed to keep to the schedule of one per month. However, the twin urges I had to take on more elaborate projects to move my own skill set forward and to keep the content on the channel fresh and interesting started to collide in an unsustainable fashion.

As I took on more and more complicated projects, the goal of getting a video out once per month became more and more remote. The resultant videos were generally well received, but it became a running joke of how infrequently I uploaded. When I originally made the Patreon I promised the videos would be "30+ minutes!" It's finally gotten to the stage where the weapons I make are baroque, can take upwards of six months to finish, and result in videos that are four hours long (I generally don't release the video until the sword is actually done). I started making smaller, if not simpler, weapons in between the longer ones to bridge the gaps, but this was time I was taking away from the main builds and was delaying their release even more. I did eventually swallow my pride and switched the Patreon from "per video" to "per month." Most of my Patreon followers were understanding, but I felt bad about doing it. I've since started taking ADHD medication. I'm hopeful I can reach some sort of equilibrium moving forward, but I guess we'll see. I've been eating into my sword-making time lately writing a book, but hopefully that turns out to be worthwhile. Like I said, I guess we'll see.

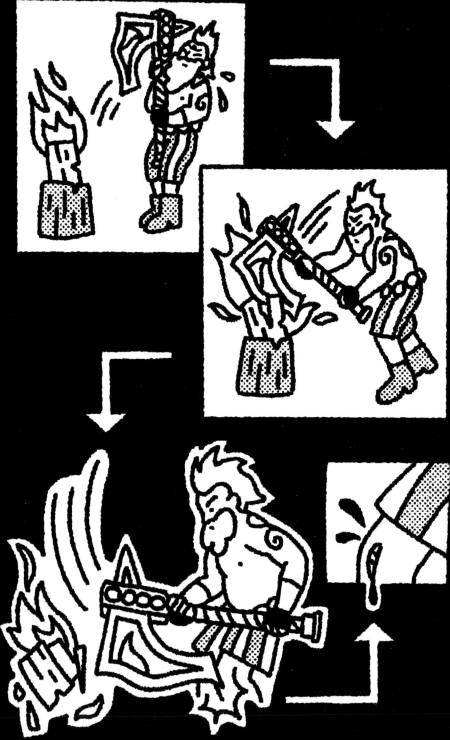

CHAPTER 9

LATHES AND THE TIMES MY SWORDS HAVE BIT ME

THERE'S A MYTH that Blackbeard set his beard on fire before getting busy with a cutlass. He didn't, but he did sometimes twist little bits of cannon fuse into his beard and light that, giving him a halo of smoke that made it look like his head was on fire. Mad lad. One of the most frequent questions I get asked is how often I set my beard on fire. The answer is not very often, but when it has happened, it doesn't burn very long. It has never erupted into a conflagration in the comedy fashion you're hoping for. If you are super unlucky, a blob of molten stuff from the plasma cutter or MIG welder will sometimes get thrown beard-ward. You hear a hiss and then get a terrible smell. The flame lasts nowhere near long enough to engage in swashbuckling.

I have had a bunch of mishaps, both with tools and swords. One of the most dangerous experiments I engage in is trying to use things as lathes that aren't lathes. Hollywood bought me a drill press, a big free-standing drill, and I very quickly did experiments mounting stuff in it other than drill bits. If I had to make a tapered handle for a blade, I'd weld a peg in the top of a big piece of bar. I'd lock that into the drill's chuck, and then use a piece of wood to make a socket the piece of bar could sit in on the drill bed. Then it was time to attack it with angle grinders. I have learned since that this approach is too wibbly wobbly to start from scratch with, so if you have the urge to copy this technique, remove as much of the material as you can BEFORE mounting it in your homemade death lathe, and then just take the final layer off in the thing that should not be. Amazingly, the worst accident I ever had with Death Lathe Mark I was getting a sanding disc too close to the edge of the spinning chuck. The chuck simultaneously ripped the sanding disc apart while sucking the grinder out of my hands. Somehow the grinder wound up somersaulting and landed on the knuckles of my left hand. The torn-up sanding disc gave them a little kiss before crashing to the floor. It didn't leave any scars, so it mustn't have been that bad, but my memory is that it sure was sting-y. Obviously, this arrangement was unsustainable, so I just eventually gave up and bought a real lathe. Nah, only kidding.

Adam of PrettyHateMachining, another YouTube channel that makes bonkers-sized weapons, presumably grimacing at what I was frequently doing, sent me a pair of small lathe chucks. The throat on one of the lathe chucks was the same as the throat on the drill chuck, so I could swap them out as needed. This arrangement was better because I could mount up much shorter, wider pieces to attack with the grinder. The only problem that presented itself was that because of the height of the drill, I was basically working upside down, bent over like an upside-down L, and my back started to complain (not unfairly). Obviously, this was silly, so I just gave up and bought a real lathe. Nah, still kidding.

The top of the drill press, the part that actually does the work, was held onto its pedestal by two screws. I undid those, thinking to lift this off the pedestal and mount it upside down in one of my step vices (I love my step vices; I never knew my real vice). The problem with that, I discovered, is the top of the drill press I had weighed well in excess of 150 pounds. The head of the drill stood about 4 feet off the ground. To free it from the pedestal, it first had to be lifted about a foot upwards, and then afterwards I had to wrestle it like the world's heaviest, most garbage blaster down into the vice, which is about 3 feet off the ground, and at some point, the whole thing had to be turned upside down. I am surprised I didn't herniate myself doing it (I am prone to herniation— we'll get into this later).

After this extremely awkward operation was carried out, the lathe chuck was much easier to use in the upright position. I could attack it like a heavy metal potter's wheel from hell. It was so much easier to use that I invested in rigging up a pulley system to make getting to the top of the pedestal drill's on and off switch more easily, using three 80-pound bags of cement as a counterweight. At this stage, even I could recognize that the lengths I was going to not use a real lathe were getting pretty silly, so I finally bought a lathe. Nah, the joke continues . . .

My Death Lathe reached final imago when I happened to notice the hole down the center of the second lathe chuck was ⅝ of an inch wide. I was at the local Martha's Vineyard dump, scavenging through their metal pile. I have never fully shaken that urge I had as a child to scavenge for *Mad Max*–type useful garbage. On this fateful day, there was a bench grinder just sitting there. You sometimes see this on the Vineyard, although it tends to be more than just one tool; it tends to be a pile of useful tools. I call them Dead Grandpa Piles. Martha's Vineyard used to be a relatively poor community before the Kennedys made it the hot spot for drowning young ladies. In a weird roundabout way, the Dead Grandpa Pile COULD represent a sort of success: "Look ghost gramps, not a single member of your venture capitalist offspring knows how to use a screwdriver. They'd rather pay some guy $100 an hour to hang a shelf!" The bad version of the Dead Grandpa Pile is that they're from houses gobbled up in a hurry during the pandemic by rich people from other families who can't afford to be on the island any more. In both universes, the contents of Grandpa's tool shed get taken to the dump and discarded unceremoniously.

I took the bench grinder home and plugged it in. It was wobbly because of some wear on the shaft. It made me a little less angry at whoever threw it out because that's a hard problem for a civilian to fix. I used J-B Weld™ to build the shaft back up and sanded carefully. I never got the chance to find out if this was a good idea or not, so I can't give you advice one way or another on that. The shaft running through the bench grinder was ⅝ inch, so I modified the second lathe chuck by drilling and tapping it so three bolts could lock it to the grinder shaft. I secured it, locked a piece of scrap steel in the chuck, and fired it up (while it was locked in a vice, of course). It worked really well until it caught fire. See, it turns out it wasn't JUST the wobbly shaft; the person who threw that bench grinder out must have been like me and used it until it was truly broken. I tried Googling the problem, and it can be caused by a short in the windings on the motor. Just running for a little while caused the motor to get insanely hot, which in turn caused the insulation on the wiring inside to combust, which can't possibly have helped. Still, even in that short time, I had proved that this was a superior method to hauling the drill everywhere. I even researched buying a new bench grinder before I noticed the broken air compressor in the corner. Sure enough, the working motor on that had a ⅝-inch spindle, and thus the modification work I did on the lathe chuck was saved.

When I used the drill as a lathe, I could set the rotation speed, and I usually set it to about 700 rpm. The bench grinder that exploded into flames spun at 1700 rpm, and the motor from the broken air compressor spun at 3400 rpm. I fitted a foot pedal AND a manual on/off switch. I won't lie, firing it up and using it is kind of terrifying, but it delivers great results. The only incident I've had with it was when a piece was mounted up incorrectly. The chuck ejected it at full speed. I wish I had filmed it. The piece had so much momentum remaining AFTER it hit one of the workshop walls that it Beybladed across the floor long enough to make me wonder if I was trapped in a Christopher Nolan film. It's the best Death Lathe I've made so far. Buy the sequel to this book to find out if it ever impacts my ability to count to ten, I guess.

As weird as it may sound though, probably the most dangerous thing about the Death Lathe is the fact that I attack what's mounted in there with an angle grinder. I have an uncommon amount of intimacy with grinders. That sounded dirtier than I meant it to. I am very skilled with an angle grinder, but as I sit here typing, naked except for the bandage on my leg, I can use the dim light reflected by the computer screen to make out three scars on my left hand from grinder kisses.

The first scar I spotted was from making Alrekr, a blood offering to the gods of metal. It sits on the top of my hand in the meat between my forefinger and thumb. I'd just been using the 9-inch grinder to put the initial rough sharpening on the blade's edge. Once the sharpening was done, I placed the turned-off, but still spinning, grinder down on a work surface. The momentum of the blade still spinning was enough to drag it off that surface. I should have let it fall; the 9-inch grinder is a big boy and could have taken a light fall, but I tried to catch it. Somehow the still spinning disc caught the back of my ungloved hand and took a big chomp out of me that seemed like it took forever to heal. I guess I learned not to try and catch falling grinders if the disc is still spinning.

The next one my eye catches is the most dramatic, starting on my forefinger knuckle and running halfway down to the next joint. The . . . five . . . (I counted) stitches are clearly visible, and they scarred up too. At Unique Designs, I learned the bad habit of removing the guard from grinders. There are a few niche applications where a guard gets in the way, advanced tricks like holding the grinder upside down and using the back of the disc to reach some hard-to-get-to spot. I was cutting a piece of bar—it wasn't even for a sword. I was using the smaller 4½-inch grinder one-handed. As previously mentioned, grinder discs are extremely brittle. This one must have had a small crack in it I couldn't see; cracked discs sometimes happen when you drop a grinder. As soon as I touched the disc off the steel, it exploded. Because of the angle in angle grinder, and the way you hold the smaller grinder one-handedly, the exploding disc is perfectly lined up to launch brittle shrapnel at your hand at a bazillion miles an hour. Furthermore, because of my grip on the grinder, the skin across that finger was stretched taut and opened up like an overripe fruit when the shattered disc hit it. I nearly fainted, not because of the pain or the blood, but because the disc must have hit a nerve or something. My finger spasmed and wouldn't close for me, making me think I had severed a tendon or the nerve itself. Luckily by the time I got to the hospital, I could move it just fine again, but once they stitched me up it was months before I could "move it just fine." I still have trouble with very specific motions, like the shoulder buttons on most game controllers. Keep your guards on your grinders!

The last one, one knuckle over, is a fifty-fifty shared responsibility between the grinder and the sword itself. As I mentioned before, when we were doing the TV show, we often had multiple copies of the same blade to show it in various stages of completion. I had a spare blank for the dog-headed sword, Cerberus, sitting uselessly in the mysterious upstairs of my workshop. I decided to finish it off and improve upon it. One of the key features of Cerberus is, instead of a blade, it has huge sharpened teeth; all the better to eat me with. The way the teeth come out of the blade, the gap between the teeth is a tricky area to grind/sharpen. I was attempting this, couched over at a weird angle, when the grinder's spinning flap disc (flaps of sandpaper) jammed between two teeth. This caused the body of the grinder to now be the spinning thing. It whipped around in my grasp and slammed the middle knuckle of my left hand into one of the already sharpened teeth. In my line of work, you get good at judging what wounds you need a Band-Aid for and what ones you need stitches for. Funnily enough, I had just gone through an anaphylactic reaction the week previous, so the ER nurses wanted to know why I was back so soon. I held up my hand to show flaps of man flesh. Be careful about your grinder disc jamming!

After the question about the burning beard, one of the other questions I get asked is about opening myself up with my swords. In general, for the amount I handle them, I think I do pretty well, but they are ridiculously heavy, sharp things, so dumb stuff does happen. The first notable scar I have from the swords themselves was because I misremembered *Don Quixote* (a figure I sometimes identify with when I'm in a more literary mood). I had misremembered that he thought the windmills were dragons, when in fact he thought they were giants. I had just finished making a sword called The Dragonslayer, a long thin isosceles trapezoid with a tapered top, and I wanted to do a bit where I attacked a windmill. I rounded up Sancho Panza (AmeriMike) and drove to Morning Glory Farms, which has a 120-foot-tall windmill for generating power. When doing stuff where there is the possibility of someone saying "No," I find the best approach is to do it as quickly as possible while pretending it has previously been arranged and apologize if there was a problem. I was talking to some employees of Morning Glory while trying to close the trunk of my car and also trying to hold The Dragonslayer. The pommel rested on my boot while the blade was crooked in my arm, and as I slammed the trunk, the pommel fell off my boot. It only traveled about 2 inches to the ground, but that was enough. The giant heavy blade slid through my elbow pit meat. Thing is, my whole act of pretending to be there with permission and that everything was chill is spoiled by me having a grievous injury, so I winced a little and then pretended it didn't happen. When I had a moment to myself, I taped it up as best I could. I didn't have bandages or anything, so it was electrical tape. You can see it in the video. I think the most embarrassing thing about the whole thing is that I got the literary reference wrong, and I think about it every time I see the scar in my left elbow. I guess the moral is not to try doing two things at once. Or to Google *Don Quixote* before role-playing him.

The most boring injury I ever received while playing with giant swords was my hernia. My father and brother also had hernias, so I guess it's genetic, but I am convinced the inciting incident for mine was a video called "Atrox the Junk Sword vs. Car." I managed to get a car that was destined for a junkyard and went to town on it. Normally, when working with my finished blades, I am very careful with how I hit them off stuff, but the whole point of Atrox was to end the debate about welded-on handles. I foolishly thought that if I made a video where I went absolutely ham on a car with a sword, it would prove what I already knew. This meant a lot of very aggressive sword use where I was purposely trying to break the handle off. Great for the experiment, but it turned out to be sucky for my groin, as I soon thereafter was diagnosed with an inguinal hernia. My favorite part of the hernia repair was the follow-up visit to the doctor two weeks later. The young doctor asked me to drop my drawers and lay back, then she exclaimed, "You said this surgery was two weeks ago? Holy moly! I've never heard of a wound healing this fast; this is incredible!" Curious, I tilted my head painfully to see what she was looking at. "Ah," I said, "You need to look lower. You are looking at my appendix scar. Sorry to disappoint."

The most dramatic injury I ever received was from a giant axe. Not only was the injury itself pretty impressive, but the whole process was captured live. The character who wields the axe in question, a dwarf named Gotrek, has a wild red mohawk. On New Year's Eve 2020, I live streamed myself getting the mohawk for charity. A very nice hair artist called Seniel Hannagan cut, styled, and dyed while money poured into a fund for Doctors Without Borders. I then donned the other parts of the costume, and it was time to try and swing the axe around. It weighed 86 pounds, and had a thicc tennis-elbow-inducing handle. I hadn't really eaten properly as I was frantically getting ready for the stream, and then when the stream started, it took about three hours to get to the point where I was actually swinging the axe around. I was exhausted after one swing or two, but the show had to go on. I arranged the usual targets: the flaming pallet and a log or two. Even then, with me being exhausted, disaster might have been avoided if I hadn't oiled the handle. Usually, oil is used to keep something safe from water or sweaty hands, but the handle of the Gotrek axe was brazed, the entire length of it, and it could have easily survived the abuse I was putting it through without the WD-40®. The oil made the handle extra slippery, exhausting me even more as I struggled to grip it.

Eventually, a very tired me tried to hit some target or other, sinking the axe into a stump. Seeing as I was exhausted, the massive axe wasn't very deep in the stump, and quickly came loose of its own accord. All 86 pounds of it fell clumsily toward the ground. This particular axe was "bearded," which meant a section of it extended down from the top of the blade, parallel to the handle.

The beard ended in a very cool-looking, but extremely pointy, spike. As the axe fell out of the stump, this spike snagged on the inside of my left knee, opening it up. Being a pro at being unzipped by this point, I knew I needed to go to the hospital immediately. I hobbled over to the live stream and ended it, leaving everyone there on a cliffhanger. I exclaimed "Hospital!" when I realized what had happened to me, and that somehow got translated to "Ambulance!" Soon the property was a circus. My cameraman, Anthony Esposito, managed to capture a lot of it on film, so it wasn't all a waste. My favorite part was when the paramedic asked me what length the blade that scragged me was. "About 2 feet," I replied. "No, no, not the handle, the blade," she clarified for me. "About 2 feet," I again insisted, as she stared at me in disbelief. There are a lot of morals in this accident, but I guess the main one is not to overexert yourself when dealing with fabulously dangerous objects.

The axe messed up my left leg, but I have written most of this book with my right leg bandaged up. As mentioned before, I discovered myself to be a late-blooming pyromaniac. One of my favorite tricks is a Molotov cocktail made with a coconut, which my friend pointed out is more of a Molotov Mai Tai. I can't believe I sometimes hit those out of the air with nothing to protect me other than a raggedy T-shirt covered in holes.

It had to catch up with me at some point, I suppose. After my marriage fell apart, I moved to Illinois, and this was my first attempt at sword-related destruction in the Midwest. My friend was nervous about throwing a Molotov Mai Tai at me without safety gear on, so I was wearing a leather coat, full leather gloves, a leather hood with a welding mask fitted to it, and my leather apron. So, my cloth work pants caught fire. Ironically, it was not because of the exploding fiery coconut I smashed out of the air with a giant sword, but because I stood in the resultant puddle of fire slightly too long. My friends rushed to put me out, but alas, they were slightly too slow. There's a bright red patch of not-skin on the back of my right calf. When it heals up, it might be the smoothest part of my body. Don't do fire-related stuff unless you are also wearing sexy leather pants, I guess.

POSTSCRIPT

IF YOU ARE READING THIS, it either means you made it all the way through my book or you're the kind of lunatic that skips to the end of a book first. Either way, I want to offer you my condolences. This is the first time I've ever written a book, so it's probably pretty garbage.

Do you want to know something gnarly that I only learned recently? Scars are a thing that have to be maintained; your body is always repairing them. When we think of pirates getting scurvy, we tend to think of their teeth falling out and so forth, but with a severe lack of vitamin C, your body can't make collagen, the glue that holds cells together. Scar tissue is even more garbage and needs more collagen than regular skin, so all the pirates' old wounds would nightmarishly pop open again and suppurate everywhere.

Writing this book, I've had to sort of put my life into review, and with that, a kind of mental scurvy set in. Some of it gets me really bone-deep tired, like going through old photos to make sure I'm not talking out of my ass about when something happened. (I used to wear a leather jacket to weld in. I stopped when it burned out and never replaced it, but it was actually a good idea, and I'm thinking about getting another.) When I think of all the effort that I wasted by not knowing the things I know now, well, like I said, I get exhausted while sitting in a chair. I've been through some big life changes recently too, so it's either a very good or really weird time to be committing to paper how I arrived at this exact point.

Sometimes people ask me will I ever stop making swords. In season one of *True Detective*, Matthew McConaughey as Reddit atheist Sigma-male Rust Cohle says, "Life's barely long enough to get good at one thing. So be careful what you get good at" (alright alright alright). And I don't even really think I'm that good at what I do! But I've invested quite a lot of time in the amount of good I am at. One of the things my ex-wife and I used to bitterly disagree about was the ability to reinvent yourself. I don't know if it is an American vs. Irish thing or what. She is a great believer in the American idea of endlessly switching careers, whereas I . . . well like I said, the Rust Cohle quote.

So, I'm "stuck" making swords from now until the final mangling I guess, and as long as I'm making them, I might as well film the process and put it on YouTube. Who knows? It might turn out that this book was woefully inadequate, and people will want a second one or whatever. I don't resent being "stuck" making videos about silly giant swords. There are plenty of worse things to be "stuck" doing, so I consider myself mostly really lucky to be in a position where you've just finished reading this sentence! You got through the whole thing!